W9-DAF-881

The Complete
Beginner's Guide to
MAGIC

The Complete Beginner's Guide to
MAGIC

Edward F. Dolan, Jr.

DOUBLEDAY & COMPANY, INC.
GARDEN CITY, NEW YORK
1977

Library of Congress Cataloging in Publication Data

Dolan, Edward F   1924–
  The complete beginner's guide to magic.

  SUMMARY: Step-by-step instructions for one hundred magic tricks, including per-
forming tips for the amateur magician.
  1. Conjuring—Juvenile literature. 2. Tricks—Juvenile literature. [1. Magic Tricks]
I. Title.
GV1548.D6   793.8
  ISBN 0-385-11554-7 Trade
        0-385-11555-5 Prebound
Library of Congress Catalog Card Number 76–56281

Copyright © 1977 by Edward F. Dolan, Jr.
  ALL RIGHTS RESERVED
  PRINTED IN THE UNITED STATES OF AMERICA
  FIRST EDITION

26043

This book is for Sharon Abbett,
who has a magic way with cards

Contents

Contents

Welcome to Magic

Magic is an art as old as mankind itself. An art that is practiced in every corner of the world. And an art that fascinates people of all ages.

There was a time when it played a key role—perhaps *the* key role—in everyday life. Many ancient peoples believed that illness was caused by writhing demons that were magically put into a man when he angered the gods. The world's first doctors were men thought to be blessed with mystical powers, men whose chants and potions could drive away the spirits of illness and death. The earliest religious leaders were men of the same kind; it was felt that their prayers could entice the gods into bringing soft rains and abundant harvests.

Similar beliefs still linger in many parts of the modern world. Voodoo and witchcraft continue to be practiced in the Caribbean area. In remote regions of Europe and Asia, old women still cook up magic recipes to insure good health, or carve amulets to keep bad luck away. Some peoples in Africa and the South Pacific will let no one photograph them, for fear that their souls will be snatched from them and imprisoned within the picture.

In most countries, however, magic is now an entertainment, a source of unending pleasure for children and adults alike. Audiences never tire of seeing rabbits pop out of a hat, coins vanish in the air, and cords mysteriously tie themselves into knots. Professional magicians are in constant demand on television and in theaters. Amateur magicians are always welcome additions to parties and local theatricals.

The purpose of this book is to let you in on all the fun by showing you how to do one hundred magic tricks. They're tricks that can be performed at the dinner table, at parties, and on the stage. They range from those that are very simple to those that are somewhat difficult. All of them are meant for the beginning magician. Some, amazingly, work by themselves. You need only follow a few easy directions, and the "magic" will do the rest.

Before talking more about the tricks themselves, let's clear up one problem. Many young people who would like to try their hand at magic are reluctant to do so. They feel that a special talent must be needed to do something as mystifying as change white handkerchiefs into colored ones or read someone's mind. And they're sure that the best tricks can be performed only with expensive and complicated equipment.

Well, nothing could be further from the truth. A special talent may be required to paint a fine picture or write a memorable poem. But no such thing is needed for you to have a wonderful time in magic and become an excellent performer. Natural ability helps, of course. But all magic tricks can be performed by *anyone* who takes the time to learn and practice them.

As for expense: Practically every trick in this book can be performed with items found in your home: playing cards, coins, string and cord, drinking glasses, matches and matchboxes, paper, handkerchiefs, and the like. Most of the tricks need not be readied ahead of time; they can be done right "on the spur of the moment." The preparation required for the others usually involves just a few seconds' or minutes' work.

In fact, in all the book, there are only four tricks that use special equipment or require lengthy preparation. They are *Blindfolded Mentalism* ☆*1*, in Chapter 8, and *Rabbit in the Box, The Silken Rainbow*, and *Ace in the Orange*, in Chapter 9. They are meant for the serious magician who wants someday to be paid for his performances. But the equipment in even these tricks has been simplified so that it can be built at home for next to nothing.

So don't worry about talent and expensive equipment. Just pitch in and have a good time.

Magic is divided into a number of branches. Our job is to look at those branches that hold the most opportunity for the beginning performer. We'll start with a chapter called "Easy Magic"; it contains tricks that can be learned about as quickly as you can read them and that are meant to build your confidence in your abilities as a magician. From there, we'll go to a chapter on more advanced card trickery.

Then we'll try our hand at tricks done with string and silk handkerchiefs. Following, there will be a chapter on "Coin Magic." If you're interested in ESP (extrasensory perception), you'll find that Chapter 8 is written especially for you; it concerns mentalism and is called "Mind Magic." And if you're interested in moving on to more serious work or to a career as a professional magician, the final chapter—"Toward Advanced Magic"—hopes to start you on your way.

Incidentally, once you're in advanced magic, you'll undoubtedly want to do more reading on the subject. You'll find much interesting material in your local library or in the Magic section of a bookstore. *The Magic Digest,* by George B. Anderson (Follett Publishing Company, Chicago), *The Amateur Magician's Handbook,* by Henry Hay (The New American Library, Inc., New York), and *Professional Magic for Amateurs,* by Walter B. Gibson (Dover Publications, Inc., New York) are among the books that should prove most helpful.

Sprinkled among our chapters, you'll find two that are meant to make you the hit of any party you attend. They're about puzzles, games, and stunts. Actually, puzzles, games, and stunts aren't magic in the true sense of the word. But there's an element of mystery to them, and professional and amateur magicians have used them for years to add some extra fun to a show or a party.

One last point: The manner in which you perform a trick is quite as important as the trick itself. Do all your actions come off smoothly? Do you convey a friendly attitude to the audience? Do you talk just enough to help the trick along and not get in its way? Do you bring off each trick with a flourish? What do you do when a trick goes wrong? To help you answer questions such as these, each trick in the book will be described in a step-by-step fashion that indicates the best way in which it can be performed. And at the ends of the chapters, you'll find short lists of advice called Performing Tips. The tips should be put to use as soon as you begin to practice the tricks.

Well, that's it. The time has come to perform.

So welcome to magic, and let's begin.

1
Easy Magic

Here are twelve tricks to start you on your way. They're beginning tricks, yes, and easy to do. But they're also something more than that.

They're very *effective* tricks. If you learn to perform them
smoothly, you'll find that they'll always amuse and baffle.
They'll win a good response from your audience and help
you to build the confidence necessary for the more advanced
magic that lies ahead. You might like some of them so much
that you'll go right on performing them for as long as you're
a magician.

The twelve are tricks that can be performed anywhere: on
stage as part of an act or at home for party fun. They all
require only the simplest household items as props. Some can
be done "on the spur of the moment," with no preparation
whatsoever. Others will need a few minutes' work ahead of
time, training you for the day when you'll be performing with
all sorts of "rigged" devices.

Magic Without Preparation
THE RESTLESS NAPKIN

All that you need for this first trick are three square paper
napkins. Two should be of one color, and the third of another. Let's say that you start with two whites and one blue.

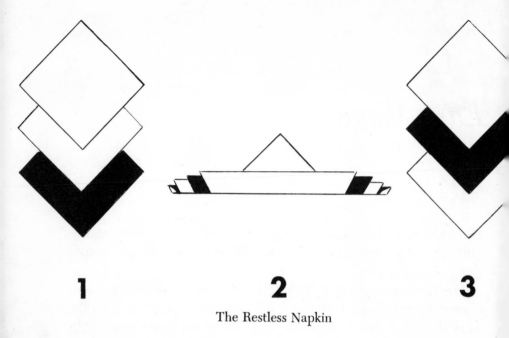

1   **2**   **3**

The Restless Napkin

Place them on a table in the staircase arrangement shown in the diagram (1). It's best to set them on a diagonal to you. This will make them easier to handle when the time comes. The blue one should be at the bottom.

Once the napkins are ready, explain that the blue one is a "restless thing." It's never happy there at the bottom. Whenever given the chance, it will insist on changing places—insist on moving up toward the top of the pile.

Your words come true when you roll the three napkins forward into a tubular shape (2) and then unroll them back toward you. Once they're flat again (3), there the blue napkin is, in the middle of the pile, lying right between the two whites.

Another forward roll—followed by an unrolling back to you—brings the blue napkin to the top of the pile.

At this point, you might insert some comedy by expressing impatience with the blue napkin and ordering it to get back where it belongs. Roll and unroll the three again. Obediently, the blue napkin returns to its place at the bottom of the pile.

The trick requires hardly any skill at all. Just roll the napkins forward until you're about an inch from the upper point of the top napkin. Because of the staircase arrangement, the upper points of the middle and bottom napkins pass beneath the tube and then flip up and over it to land on the top napkin. Let the two of them flip. Then stop and unroll. The two flips actually rearrange the order of the napkins. The top napkin moves to the bottom of the pile and the blue one to the middle.

Try the roll for yourself. You'll see exactly how the two flips alter the positions of the napkins.

Repeat the roll, count two flips, and unroll; the top napkin is gone and the blue is in its place. A third roll and two flips now drop the blue to its original spot at the bottom.

The trick can be altered in several ways. One flip jumps the blue napkin all the way from the bottom of the pile to the top. Another flip takes it down a single step from the top to the middle. Three flips leave the napkins just as they were at the start of a roll. If you memorize what the various flips do, you can literally cause the napkin to jump all about in the pile.

CHAIN LIGHTNING

This is a trick that works automatically. You needn't do a thing except follow the steps below. You'll amaze yourself.

Borrow a dollar bill or a rectangular sheet of paper from a friend. Fold it into an S shape and attach two paper clips to it in the manner shown in the photo. Hold the bill up for everyone to see and then pull it out straight. The clips hop into the air and fly about two or three feet out in front of you. When your friend picks them up, he finds—miracle of miracles!—that they're joined together.

You can add to the fun by hanging the two joined clips to

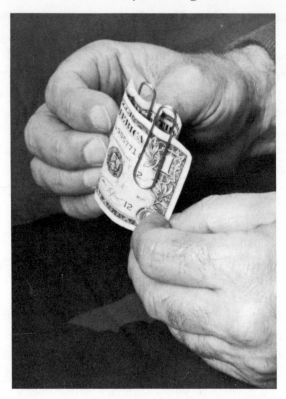

Chain Lightning

one side of the bill and a third to the other. The three clips will join when you pull the bill straight. You can carry on from there and fashion the clips into a long chain or, alternatively, a pendant.

THE CHRISTMAS TREE

Many magicians consider *The Christmas Tree* to be just about the best paper trick in magic. When the tree is fashioned of fancy gift wrapping or brightly colored wallpaper, it makes a fine addition to a holiday performance. The tree can also be made of several sheets of newspaper taped end to end and still be a very attractive presentation.

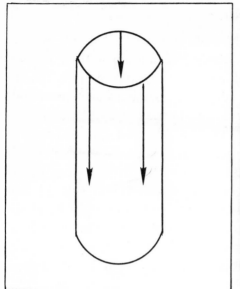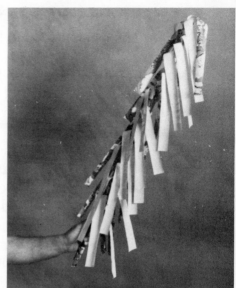

The Christmas Tree

Roll the paper into a tube and secure it with a rubber band at one end. Next, starting from the opposite end, make the three scissors cuts shown in the diagram. They should go no farther down the tube than its midway point. Once the cuts are made, remove the rubber band, reach into the tube at the top, take the paper there between your fingers, and very gently begin to pull it upward.

Slowly, as seen in the photograph, the tree takes shape, with the strips of paper cascading outward to form the branches. Continue pulling upward until the top "branches" are out of reach. The tree can then be nursed the rest of the way to its full height by pushing it upward from its base leaves.

When the tree is completed, why not give it to someone in the audience as a gift? Or perhaps stand it in a flowerpot. A piece of mailing tube about three inches long and fastened to a circular cardboard base should be placed in the flowerpot. The device can be made in just a few minutes and will serve to keep the tree standing straight.

THE JUMPING RUBBER BAND

The rubber band that helped you with *The Christmas Tree* can now be used to startle the audience. Just slip it around the base of your index and middle fingers. Then, with a sudden movement of your hand, send the band "jumping" over to circle your ring and little fingers.

It's all done simply. First (Picture A), hold up the back of your right hand to the audience and slip the rubber band into place. Next (Picture B), stretch the band a few times with your left hand as if checking its elasticity. But on the final pull (Picture C), bend the fingers of your right hand so that they all go inside the area formed by the stretched band. Finally (Picture D), release the band from your left hand and straighten the fingers of your right hand at the same time.

The band will now be around your ring and little fingers.

You complete the trick by having the band jump back to your index and middle fingers. Slip your thumb under the band (Picture E) and pull it outward. Drop your fingers into the opening made by the band (Picture F). Release the band from your thumb. Back it will jump to your index and middle fingers.

Make the band jump back and forth as often as you wish. If you work smoothly and quickly, and with the back of your hand always to the audience, the spectators will never sight the finger movements that make the trick possible.

TWO FOR ONE

Here's a trick that's especially suitable for the dinner table. Place your hands flat on the table—palms up and about an inch apart—and have a guest drop a coin into each hand. Pause for a moment for dramatic effect. Then, without lifting your hands, flip them quickly over toward each other. Bring your palms flat against the table, put on an innocent face, and ask:

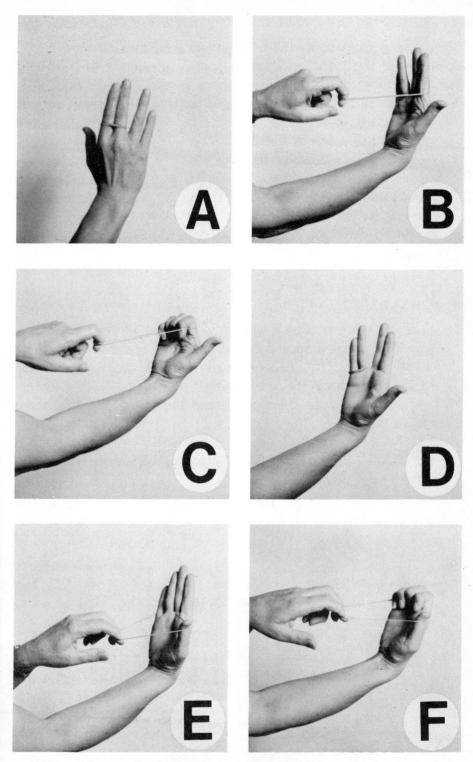

The Jumping Rubber Band

"How many coins do I have under each hand?"

Your audience will swear that you simply turned your hands over and so must still have a coin beneath each one. But, if you're right-handed, *both* coins will be under the *left* hand when you reveal them.

With just a few moments' practice, *Two for One* works automatically. Because of its extra strength, your right hand always throws its coin over to the left just before your turning left hand comes flat against the table. The trick works in reverse for left handers.

Now, while you've got coins on the table, let's try another money trick:

THE OBEDIENT COINS

The Obedient Coins can be performed for people of any age, but it has a special charm for small children. They'll be captivated by it, particularly if you talk coaxingly to the coins throughout the whole routine, pleading with them to do what you want them to do and then congratulating them when they obey.

The trick must be done on a table that is covered with a tablecloth. First (Picture *A*), place two quarters on the ta-

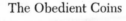

The Obedient Coins

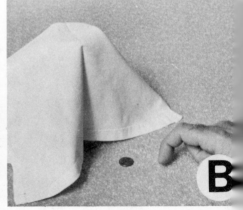

blecloth, set a drinking glass upside down on them, and push two pennies under the mouth of the glass. Then cover the glass with a handkerchief. Make certain that the edges of the handkerchief just touch the tablecloth or hang free of it by a fraction of an inch.

All set? Now (Picture *B*) call for the first of two coins to "come out and see everyone." With the tip of your index finger, begin to scratch the tablecloth a few inches in front of the glass. Continue to tell the coin to "come out." At first, nothing will happen. Have the children join in, begging the coin to obey. In about fifteen seconds or so, it will appear from under the edge of the handkerchief and move to you.

Pick it up, thank it for being a "good coin," and then call for the second one to come out, scratching the tablecloth as you do so. It will "obey" in another fifteen or so seconds.

The magic behind the trick? The movement of the tablecloth caused by the scratching action of your index finger.

Magic Needing Preparation

PRESTO! A KNOT

Perhaps one day you'll be attempting tricks with devices that need long and careful preparation before you dare take them on stage. But for now, right at the start of your work in magic, here's a trick that actually takes longer to perform than to prepare.

Produce a silk handkerchief from your pocket or purse and dangle it from the fingertips of your right hand. Next, promising your audience that you'll form a knot in the dangling end with a single flick of your wrist, bring the dangling end up with your left hand so that your right hand can take it. Then give the handkerchief a firm snap with your right hand and release one end. And there the knot will be, at the dangling end.

The preparation: Before you go onstage, simply tie a small knot in one corner of the scarf. When you produce the scarf, be sure to hide the knot beneath the fingers of your right hand. Then, after you've brought the unknotted end to your right hand, continue to hold it in place as you snap your wrist. Release the knotted end. If performed smoothly, the knot will give the appearance of flowing down through the handkerchief to the dangling end.

So that the trick could be easily explained, we formed the knot on the first flick of your wrist. You can make the trick look more difficult—and add to the fun—by releasing the un-knotted end on your first two tries and seeming frustrated because the trick appears to be failing. But on your third try —there the knot is.

If you don't have a scarf, a large handkerchief will do just as well. Needless to say, this trick can be performed just once. If you wish, you can use it as a "filler"—a bit of magic meant to entertain audiences for a moment or two between more serious tricks.

THE CARD FINDER

In Chapter 3, we'll be talking about card tricks. To ready you for them, let's try one of the simplest but most baffling of their number. It requires just a minimum of preparation.

Place six cards in two rows as seen in Picture A. Then turn away and ask a friend to reverse one of them—swing it around so that its ends change places. When you face the table again, the cards may look as they do in Picture B. Gaze at them thoughtfully for a moment and then point to the reversed card.

The secret behind the trick? It's right there in Pictures A and B. You'll see it for yourself if you'll study the cards for a few moments.

Got it?

The *three of clubs* is the reversed card. In Picture A, two of its spots are pointing toward the top of the card, while

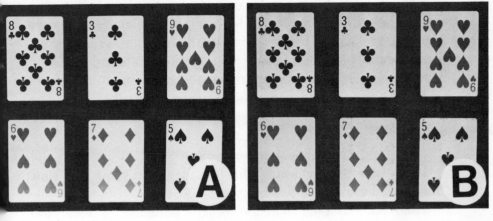

The Card Finder

one is pointing toward the bottom, but in Picture *B*, the two
spots are pointing toward the bottom—a dead giveaway that
the card has been reversed.

The six cards are known as "pointers," meaning that they
have more spots pointing in one direction than the other. To
identify any reversed pointer card, you need only know the
direction in which most of its spots were pointing at the start
of the trick.

There are nineteen pointers in any deck of cards. To prepare for the trick, just select six of their number and place
them at the top of the deck. If you plan to repeat the trick
with new cards, then add an appropriate number to the original six.

You can perform the trick without preparation if you wish.
But it's best to ready things ahead of time. Then you can
peel the cards off and lay them out without delay. You won't
need to search through the deck for six pointers and give
away the fact that the trick uses special cards.

The pointer cards are to be found in three suits: clubs,
hearts and spades. They are the *three, five, six, seven, eight,*
and *nine*. The seven of diamonds is also a pointer; if you'll
check the figures above, you'll see that the center diamond is
closer to one end of the card than the other. You may also

use the ace of clubs, hearts, or spades as pointers, but they really should be avoided; it's too easy for the audience to see that an ace points in the opposite direction when reversed. The spectators then become suspicious of the other cards, start looking at them closely, and soon "catch on" to the secret behind the trick.

MAGIC MATCHES ※ 1

Long enough for some glue to dry: that's all the time you'll need to prepare this puzzler.

Hold up a box of matches for the audience to see. Push open the box at one end to show the heads of the matches. Open the other end and display the bottoms. Ask the audience to remember at which end of the box the heads are located.

Now comes the fun as you cause the heads to "hop" back and forth from one end of the box to the other. Push open the end of the box where the bottoms of the matches should be; magically, the heads will be there. Close the box and immediately push open the end where the heads should be; and there they are! Keep opening each end of the box. The heads will always appear.

To prepare for the trick, remove a number of matches from the box and cut them in half. The halves containing the heads are then arranged in a row and glued to a small sheet of cardboard or stiff paper. When the rigged matches are put back in the partially filled box, their heads should be placed above the bottoms of the real matches.

Begin the trick by showing the audience the heads of the real matches. But just before displaying the bottoms of the matches, tilt the box, causing the rigged matches to slide down over the real heads and out of sight; this tilting movement is a natural one and won't arouse anyone's suspicion. For the rest of the trick, just keep tilting the box back and forth so that the real and fake heads are always seen when the box is opened.

MAGIC MATCHES ⚡2

A similar trick can be done with even less preparation.

Again, hold up a matchbox. Push it open at either end to show that the matches within are just ordinary ones. Then, holding the box in one palm, pass your other hand over it and give the matches the power to "defy gravity." Remove the cover from the box and turn the drawer upside down.

Indeed, the matches do defy gravity. They refuse to fall!

If this isn't enough magic for you, give another wave of your hand and remove the "gravity-defying power." Out tumble the matches in a shower.

The trick is prepared by cutting one of the matches to the width of the drawer and then wedging it in crosswise on top of the others so that it holds them in place. It should be placed midway along the box to avoid the danger of being seen when you first open the box at either end.

After the matches have defied gravity for a moment or so, you let them fall by pressing your fingers against the sides of the drawer near its bottom. The sides flare and release the wedge.

Incidentally, collect the matches and put them away as soon as they've fallen. Otherwise, some sharp eye may see that one of them is shorter than the others.

THE MAGIC MATCHBOX

Want to try another matchbox trick? A bit of mechanical skill is needed to prepare this one.

Produce your matchbox and remove the cover. Display the cover from all angles to prove that there is nothing unusual about it. Next, pass a string through the cover, invite two spectators to come on stage, and have them hold the ends of the string, with the cover hanging midway along its length. Now drape a silk scarf over the box and say a few magic words.

The climax of the trick comes when you reach under the scarf and bring your hand back out with the matchbox cover

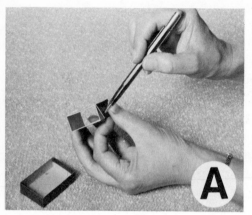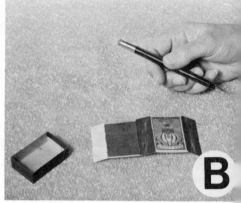

The Magic Matchbox

in it. Left behind is the string, still hanging there undisturbed between the two spectators.

The preparation: When you look at a matchbox cover from either end, you'll see that one of its sides is made of two pieces of wood glued together (Picture A). Cut along the base of these pieces so that they come apart and the cover opens (Picture B). A daub of paste or beeswax is now used to hold them together until the moment when you reach beneath the scarf. With your hand concealed, force the two pieces of wood apart with your thumbnail. Once the cover is free of the string, press the pieces together again and bring out the cover. And the audience will think it's all magic!

READ THE COIN

A moment of preparation and a simple hand action are the main ingredients in *Read the Coin.* But if you present the trick dramatically, you can turn it into a few moments of extrasensory perception (ESP) that your audience will long remember.

Start by borrowing a nickel from a friend. He is to hold it in his fist for a moment and press it as hard as he can. Then he is to drop it into the palm of your right hand. Close your hand immediately into a fist, hiding the coin from view.

Now the dramatics begin. Tell the audience that, when your friend held the coin, he activated certain electrical impulses in it, some of which passed into his fingers. You are very sensitive to such vibrations. With your friend's help, you will now allow those vibrations to pass into your brain. They will permit you to see the coin mentally—and so clearly that you'll be able to call out the date printed on it.

Have your friend stand in front of you and lightly press his fingertips against your forehead. Place your fist with the coin in it against the back of your neck. Concentrate deeply as the impulses in the coin and the fingertips "pass into" your brain. Tell the audience that you have a beginning impression of the coin, that it's growing clearer, and that finally it's as clear as can be. You can actually see the date! Call it out slowly.

Return the coin to your friend and have him read the date aloud.

It will be the date that you called.

Well, unless you're very fortunate, you're not blessed with ESP. So how do you do it?

To start with, you've got a nickel of your own. It's hidden in a pocket that's convenient to reach. Of course, you've taken the time beforehand to memorize its date.

As your friend is holding his nickel in his fist, casually reach into your pocket and take your coin in your right hand (left, if you're left-handed). Conceal the coin by holding it against your palm with your bent ring and little fingers. You'll find it quite easy to take the coin in your hand and grasp it in this fashion.

Your ring and little fingers remain folded over when your friend drops his nickel into your hand. You may worry that your hand looks a little strange. But if you immediately close the rest of your fingers into a fist, your friend won't have the chance to think that anything is wrong.

Now, when you bring your fist to the back of your neck during the final part of the trick, your fingers come right against your neck, with your thumb turned down naturally toward your collar. All that you do now is open your thumb and index finger slightly. Your friend's nickel drops inside your collar. You're left with your coin—the one whose date you've memorized and that you now hand to your friend.

If you've enjoyed this bit of ESP, then you'll really have a good time with the "mind magic" tricks in Chapter 8.

Performing Tips

1. Though these beginning tricks are simple ones, they need to be practiced before being tried on an audience. You'll be eager to test them on your friends, but keep a rein on your impatience. Only when you've got everything down pat will it be time for a public showing. There's nothing worse than to present a half-learned trick and forget what comes next when you're in the middle of it.

2. You'll be concentrating hard on what you're doing when practicing and presenting your first tricks. But don't forget about the *manner* of your presentation. Develop a good line of talk—"patter"—to go along with the tricks. It should help the audience follow the tricks, but should never give your secrets away. Be friendly and natural in your talk. And talk just enough to keep the tricks going and the audience entertained. Too much patter can smother a trick.

3. A few tricks in magic may be repeated once or twice. Most, however, should be presented just *once*. Otherwise, you run the risk of boring the audience and giving your secrets away.

4. Many of your friends will want to know how a trick works. Don't offend them, but don't tell them. The way tricks are done is the best kept of the magician's secrets.

5. Now that you've read the chapter, you may want to begin assembling some tricks into an act. If so, choose six or seven that please you most. Begin your act with a very short trick so that the audience's attention is immediately captured. Then alternate between short and longer tricks. End with your very best trick.

2
First Card Magic

It is believed that playing cards were invented in early India or China. For centuries now, they have been responsible for countless tricks. Today, because these tricks remain as baffling and as entertaining as ever, the magician always has several of them on hand, ready for use. In fact, many a magician builds his entire act—even his entire career—around card magic.

As is true of all magic, the tricks that pop out of a deck of cards range from the simple to the difficult. Some can be done without preparation and some must be carefully readied beforehand. Some require great manual dexterity; others can be performed by magicians who can do no more than shuffle the cards.

This is the first of two chapters on this fascinating branch of magic. In it, you'll find the simplest of tricks. They all need just a minimum of skill. A later chapter will go into more advanced trickery.

The tricks in this chapter begin with five that will amaze even you as the magician. They're tricks that work by themselves. You need do no more than follow the steps described below. The mathematics and the arrangement of the fifty-two cards will take over from there.

Card Tricks That Work by Themselves

ALL FOUR-OF-A-KIND

Separate all the suits in the deck. With the help of one or two spectators, arrange the cards in each suit in successive order—from the ace through the king. Place the four suits together, one on top of the other, and have a friend cut the pack as often as he pleases. Do not allow the deck to be shuffled, just cut.

Once the deck is well cut, deal the cards one at a time around the table into thirteen piles of four cards each. Collect the cards, put them together, and then deal off *four cards* at a time until you again have thirteen piles. Have your friend now turn each of the piles face up. He'll be astonished to find that each contains cards all of the same value. All the kings will be together, as will all the other cards right down through the ace.

The trick never fails, because the cuts always maintain the order of the cards. Try a few sample cuts for yourself and see. One caution, however: each cut should be a single one; that is, the deck should be divided in two and the lower portion put on top of the upper portion before the next cut. Some people like to divide the deck into three heaps when cutting. This destroys the arrangement of the cards.

THE FRIENDLY TRIO

Here's another trick in which numerous cuts fail to alter the arrangement of the cards. It begins when you remove three of the aces from the deck and hand them to a friend.

Next, after setting the deck on the table, instruct him to return the aces to it, placing one on the top, one on the bottom, and one in the middle. Once they're in place, your friend may cut the deck as often as he pleases. Single cuts only. No shuffling.

Now flip the deck over on its back and fan it out on the table. There the three aces will be—miraculously together after the numerous cuts seemed to mix the cards so thoroughly.

How's it done? When you remove the aces at the start, gather all four. But secretly place one at the bottom of the deck before passing the others to your friend. When he then returns one of the three to the bottom, it will join the ace already there. The first cut will bring the top ace to a position beneath its two friends. Three aces will be together and should remain together no matter the number of cuts now made. The chances that your friend will separate the aces by cutting between them are very remote. If he does, make a joke of it and repeat the trick.

The secretly placed ace, of course, makes up one of the trio. Its suit will be different from the three given to your friend. But unless he has the sharpest eyes in the world, he won't notice this little oddity.

CARD CALCULATOR ⚹ 1

Have a friend take a card without letting you see it. Let's say that he chooses the *five of diamonds*. He is now to multiply its value by *3;* then add *6* to the total; and end by dividing the result by *3*. Ask him to give you his final total.

Immediately, you name the value of the card: five.

Involved is the simplest of arithmetic. Five multiplied by *3* is *15;* *6* added to *15* comes to *21;* and *21* divided by *3* leaves *7.* Your friend does all the work and you take all the credit by merely subtracting *2* from *7* to reach the value of his card.

The subtraction of *2* from your friend's final total will always yield the value of his card, no matter what it may be. Try it yourself and see.

But what if your friend takes an ace or a picture card? There will be no problem if you give these cards number values at the start of the trick. Aces count as *1;* jacks as *11,* queens as *12,* and kings as *13.*

MAGIC TWENTY-ONE

Magic Twenty-one begins when you lay out three rows of seven cards each (Picture A). Ask a friend to pick a card in one of the rows. He is not to name the card aloud but is only to tell you the row in which it is. We'll pretend that he picks the *ace of clubs,* which is in row 1.

Pick up the three rows. As you do so, place your friend's row *between* the other two. Turn the pile of cards face down and again deal them out into three rows, dropping them face up as you go along. At the start of the trick, you might have dealt the cards straight down each row, but now deal them from the left to the right; that is, start at the top of row 1, move to the top of row 2, then go to row 3, come back to row 1, and continue in the same way from there. When the cards are all in place, have your friend tell you in which row his card is now located. It's jumped over to row 3 (Picture B).

Once again, pick up the cards, placing row 3 between rows 1 and 2. Turn the pile face down and, dealing from left to right, build three new rows. As before, deal the cards out face up.

For the last time, have your friend point out the row in which his card is situated, now row 1 (Picture C). Gather up the cards, this time with row 1 in the middle.

Now for the finish: Slowly count off ten cards, placing them face down and one at a time in front of your friend. Pause just before the eleventh card and predict that his card will be the next to appear.

Turn it over. True to your words, it's the ace of clubs!

If you look closely at the final illustration, you'll discover the secret behind the trick. No matter what card your friend has picked, it will end up in the middle of its row on the third deal, with three cards above it and three cards below it. The mathematics of the twenty-one cards always places it there.

When you pick up the rows for the last time, you know

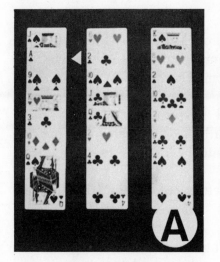

Magic Twenty-one

that the selected card is separated from the top by ten cards —seven in the topmost row, plus three in its own row. You only have to deal out ten cards and then turn the eleventh over to seem a wizard.

CARD CALCULATOR #2

After shuffling the deck thoroughly, ask a friend to deal the cards face up into a number of rows while you are turned away or out of the room. He is, however, to set the cards out in a certain way.

Let's say that the first card he turns up is the *seven of spades*. He counts the next card as 8 and the following one as 9. He continues counting until he reaches 12. A new row must now be started.

Suppose it begins with a picture card. Your friend counts the card as 10. The next is 11, followed by 12. The second row is at an end.

Your friend continues counting out the rest of the cards in the same manner. Let's say that he completes six rows and then, with six cards left, turns over the three of hearts. Not enough cards remain to reach 12. His counting stops at this point. The rows and the six cards look as they do in Picture A.

Your friend then gathers up each row, squares it off neatly, and turns it face down. When doing so, he must not alter the arrangement in any row. He then places his six remaining cards in a face-down fan below the rows. When you return to the table, the cards look as they do in Picture B.

Now comes the point of the trick: You have X-ray eyes (at least, that's what you tell the audience). You can look right through the backs of the top cards in the six rows. To prove it, you'll add up the values of the top cards. Your answer is guaranteed to be correct.

Stare thoughtfully at the cards for a moment and then announce that the total is 32. Turn each top card over, counting as you go along. On the final card up (Picture C), the total will be—just as you said it would—32.

It's all done mathematically, of course. Begin by counting the number of rows—six in all in this instance. Next, subtract 4 from this number, leaving 2. Then multiply 2 by 13, for a total of 26. Finish off by adding the number of fanned cards —six—to 26. And there you are with 32!

Card Calculator ※2

Use the same formula no matter the number of rows and the number of remaining cards. Your friends will be sure that you're a mathematical genius.

HANDLING THE CARDS

Every card magician must be able to handle the deck with ease and confidence. So, before going any further, let's pause to talk about the first basic of card manipulation: the shuffle.

The shuffle, of course, mixes the cards thoroughly in games so that there is no chance of a player's cheating. In magic, it convinces the audience that you're not arranging the cards in any special order for a trick. But, as you'll see in a moment, it also helps you to perform certain tricks; in fact, unless you're able to shuffle easily, you'll find certain tricks quite difficult, if not impossible, to master. The shuffles used in magic are the same as those found in games: the *riffle* and the *overhand*.

The riffle shuffle is often called the *dovetail*. Take roughly half the deck in each hand and hold the cards in the manner shown in Picture A. Just release the inner edges of the cards one at a time so that the two halves come together, with the cards meeting and dovetailing. The shuffle ends when you

The Riffle and Overhand Shuffles

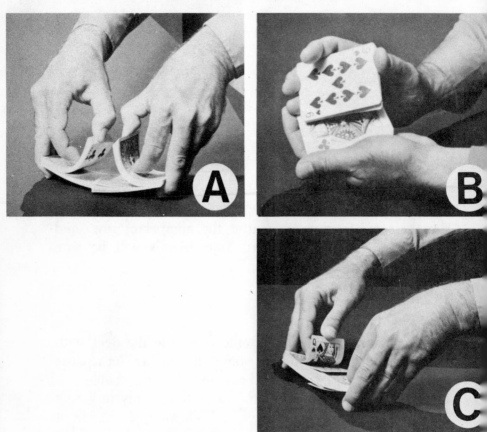

push the interlaced cards toward each other and square the deck neatly.

Throughout, try to keep the cards as close to the table as possible. Never hold the deck so that the bottom cards are flashed to the audience. You'll know why soon.

To perform the overhand shuffle, hold the cards as shown in Picture *B*. Then lift small clusters of cards from the back of the deck and drop them in front of the deck. You may also take small clusters from the middle or drop small clusters into the middle. The shuffle may be reversed, with the cards being lifted from the front of the deck and then being deposited at the back.

How can the ability to shuffle help you perform a trick? In many tricks, you'll need to know the bottom card in the deck. In others, you'll need to know the top card. These cards can be pretty easily seen whenever you shuffle (Picture *C*), but they can be seen at a *glance* if you are able to shuffle well. You need not shuffle slowly for fear of missing them, nor need you bend down to peer at the deck. In fact, you can sight them so quickly that your audience won't be aware of what you're doing.

Before trying the next trick, it would be a good idea to practice shuffling for a few minutes. For the trick can't be done unless you glimpse the bottom card. Once you master this one, you'll be ready for the top- and bottom-card routines that are waiting for you in the chapter on more advanced card magic.

Easy Card Magic

SEE THROUGH THE DECK

In this one, your X-ray vision seems to be at work once more.

Shuffle the deck and hold it for a moment behind your back. Bring it out and extend it to the front as shown (Picture *A*), with the bottom card facing toward a friend so that

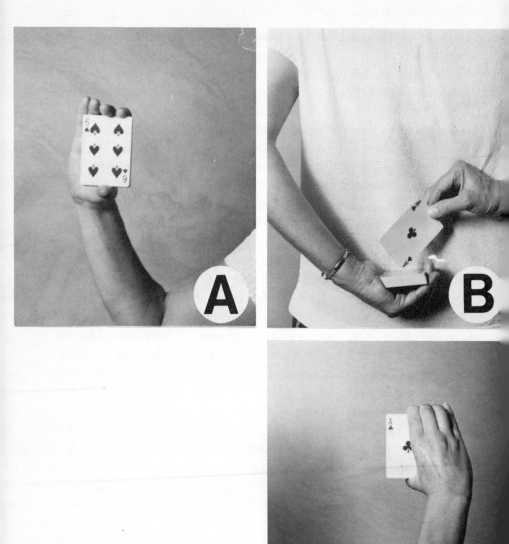

See Through the Deck

you can't possibly see it. To make sure that no one accuses you of peeking at the card as you produce the deck, close your eyes momentarily.

Then look right at your friend and startle him by naming the bottom card.

Again hold the deck behind you. Bring it out once more with a new bottom card. Again name the bottom card. Continue "seeing through the deck" for as long as it mystifies and entertains your friend.

The trick is done in two steps. First, while either riffle or overhand shuffling, catch a glimpse of the bottom card. Suppose it's the *six of spades*. Memorize it and you'll have completed the first step. You're all set to name the initial bottom card that you'll show to your friend.

Now the second step:

Once the cards are behind your back, leave the six of spades in place. But turn over the top card on the deck (Picture *B*). In this case, it's the *ace of clubs*. Then, during the time you hold the deck to the front and call off the six, look at and memorize the ace (Picture *C*).

Once your hands are again behind you, transfer the ace to the bottom of the deck and turn over the card that is now at the top. Repeat this action each time the deck goes behind your back.

CARD MEMORY

Now that you've had a chance to practice with the bottom card, we'll relax a bit. As said before, we'll have more top- and bottom-card tricks later, but for the time being let's try what is called a "pattern" trick. The pattern here is based on four secret words.

Draw ten pairs of cards from the deck and place them face up on the table. Have several friends each mentally select a pair. Then, making sure not to separate the pairs, gather up the cards and set them out face down into four rows of five cards each. Do not build each row in turn. Rather, hop about, seeming to place the cards at random.

Once the cards are in place, turn away or leave the room. Each friend then peeks beneath the cards and writes on a sheet of paper the rows in which his pair is situated. When you return, glance at the paper and then turn up two cards for each friend. The correct pair is produced every time.

But how?

Though you seem to set the cards out at random, you actually follow a certain pattern. To follow that pattern, just imagine that four words of five letters each are printed on the table, one directly under the other:

A T L A S

T H I G H

G O O S E

B I B L E

If you'll look closely at the words, you'll see that, together, they contain ten pairs of letters: A-A, T-T, L-L, and so on. As you lay out the cards, you do no more than place the cards of each pair on corresponding letters. Start with *A* and place the first pair in the top row, with two spaces between them. The second pair (T-T) goes in the first and second rows. The third pair (L-L) belongs in the first and fourth rows. Then just continue through the paired letters until all the cards are in place.

When a friend then writes that his cards are in the second and third rows, you know that you must pick cards up from the two *G* positions. If the pair is in the third row, you know it's in the *O* positions.

If you try this trick more than once and always set the cards out in the same order, someone will soon realize that you're following a pattern. With a little practice, you'll be able to alter the pattern, perhaps starting at the bottom with the *B* positions and then working up from there. In time, you'll be able to start anywhere in the pattern and still complete it successfully.

Or, if you prefer, you can change the words. For instance, you might try:

```
C O L O R
U S U A L
S H E E R
C H A F F
```

Or:

```
B A S E S
L A R R Y
T I T L E
B I F F Y
```

CHOSEN CARD UP

Chosen Card Up is what is known as a reversal trick. While you hold the deck face down, a friend takes a card, secretly shows it to his fellow spectators, and returns it to the deck. When you then spread the deck out on the table, the chosen card is found to have reversed itself. Miraculously, it's turned itself over on its back and is lying face up (Picture A).

The trick is made possible by two seemingly innocent moves

Chosen Card Up

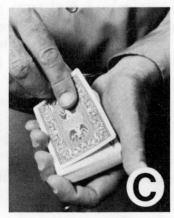

on your part. The first move begins when your friend takes a card. Immediately turn away from him, making the excuse that you don't want to risk seeing his card as he shows it to the rest of the audience. But once your back is safely to him, turn the deck over in your hands as shown below and then turn the topmost card face down (Pictures *B* and *C*).

When you swing around to the audience again, it will seem as if nothing has happened to the deck. So that the cards won't be jostled and reveal the fact that only the top card is face down, hold the deck firmly as your friend inserts his card. Now for your second move: turn away again, saying that you're giving him the chance to whisper the name of his card to anyone who may have forgotten it. Quickly turn the top card face up and then turn the deck over in your hand.

Now you're ready for the finish. All the cards are turned face down—except one. When the deck is spread out, there the chosen card will be, face up.

CARD TOUCH ✸ 1

A few pages ago, your X-ray vision enabled you to see through the backs of the cards to the spots on the other side. Now how about a trick that lets you "see" a card not with your eyes but with your fingertips?

Begin by turning away and asking several friends each to take a card from the deck and place it on the table. Once the cards have been selected, seat yourself in front of your friends. Take each card as it is now handed to you face down and hold it in one hand in the manner shown so that you can't see the face. Then rub the face gently with the forefinger of your other hand.

Obviously, your sense of touch is magical, for you're able to name each card correctly.

The photograph reveals the secret to the trick. As you rub the face with your forefinger, apply a bit of pressure and bend the card slightly. The bend, which will seem quite natu-

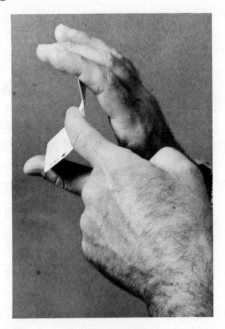

Card Touch #1

ral to your friends, permits you to see the card's identifying corner mark.

You and your magic sense of touch!

CARD TOUCH #2

Here's another trick that seems to be done by magic touch alone. Square the deck neatly, hold it in your palm, and have a friend lift a number of cards from the top. The cards should be removed in a single group so that you have no chance of seeing how many are being taken.

Keeping the remainder of the deck in your hand, turn away while your friend silently counts his cards. Let's say that they total nineteen.

Turn again and have him replace his cards on top of the deck in your palm. Cup your hands about the deck. Pretend to feel it thoughtfully. At last, place the deck on a table and cut a number of cards from it in a single group.

When your friend counts them, he'll find that they number nineteen.

The secret? While your friend is counting his cards, cup your hand hard and press the remainder of the deck into a slight bend. When the nineteen cards are returned to you, there will be an almost undetectable opening between them and the rest of the deck. To return the nineteen cards to your friend, feel for the opening when you cut the deck.

When you first practice the trick, you may have a little trouble finding the opening. Experience will quickly take care of this.

Performing Tips

1. When practicing the tricks in this chapter, be sure to spend some time just shuffling and handling the cards. Learn to manipulate the cards easily and smoothly so that you never delay a trick by dropping, bending, or tangling them.

2. Once you've become adept at card manipulation, don't "show off" your ability. If your actions seem to be saying, "Look how good I am," you'll only irritate your audience. Further, should you then drop the cards or make some other mistake, you'll look particularly foolish.

3. Though card tricks are fun at a party, they can tire quickly if continued too long. Watch your friends closely. If they're enjoying it all, carry on. But if they're growing restless, it's time to stop.

4. If you're performing on a stage—whether doing card tricks or any other kind of magic—limit yourself to no more than eight or ten minutes. Then, should you be called back for an encore, do just one or two quick tricks, even though you think everyone wants you to go on entertaining all night. There's an old saying in the entertainment field that every new performer should memorize and never forget: "Always leave the audience wanting more."

5. Some card tricks can be repeated at parties without revealing their secrets or boring your friends; repeat them just as few times as possible. When performing on stage, present each of your tricks just *once*. Repeats tire the audience, eat up too much time, and reduce the number of other tricks that can be done before it's time to bow and leave.

3
Puzzle and Game Magic

Now, as promised at the beginning of the book, here's a special brand of magic for you. It doesn't involve the magician's usual trickery. You don't name a secret card, cause matches to defy gravity, or have a string tie a knot in itself. Rather, you entertain your audience in quite another way.

You have them work puzzles that, at first glance, seem to have no solution. You challenge them to games. Some they can win, and some they can't no matter how hard they try. Altogether, your friends have a fine time scratching their heads and being thoroughly frustrated.

These puzzles and games are easy to learn and do. Some can be incorporated into a magic act as tricks or as "fillers" to entertain between tricks. All can be used "on the spur of the moment" at parties, for they require no special props or preparation. They have been known to keep guests happily mystified for an entire evening.

In this chapter, there are sixteen examples of puzzle and game magic. We'll start with some puzzles. So that you can have the fun of working them out for yourself, let's withhold their solutions until the end of the chapter.

Puzzles

CARDS CROSS

This is one of the oldest of puzzles. And one of the simplest. Yet it always stumps the players for a time. Some never figure it out.

Arrange six cards in the form of a cross, with four cards running vertically and three horizontally. Then challenge a friend to rearrange them in *one* move so that the vertical and horizontal lines each contain four cards.

If you're without a deck of cards, the puzzle can be just as easily done with seven coins or slips of paper.

Give it a try. Figured it out yet?

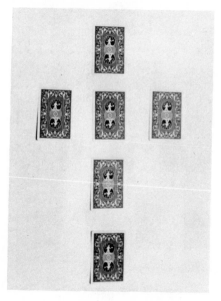

Cards Cross Setup

TWO-BY-FOUR

You need just eight matches to frustrate a friend completely. Challenge him to form them into *two* squares and *four* triangles.

Two-by-Four quickly becomes a game when several friends are given matches and pitted against each other in a race. The first one to come up with the simple (but very tricky) solution is declared the winner—and is given the matches as a prize.

TURN-AROUND TRIANGLE

Now that you've got your audience thinking about triangles, why not set out ten playing cards in the arrangement shown?

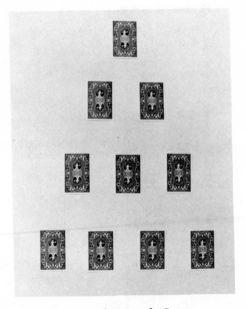

Turn-around Triangle Setup

The challenge?
Turn the triangle around so that it is pointing in the opposite direction. But do so by moving just *three* cards.

SUBTRACTING SQUARES

From triangles let's get back to squares for a moment. Arrange twenty toothpicks or matches in the design shown.

Subtracting Squares

Then say:

"There are seven squares here. Can you rearrange the matches so that they form just five squares? All twenty matches must be in your final design. The squares must all be of the same size."

You don't have to say any more. In fact, it will do no good to talk further. Your friends will be too busy to listen.

FOUR SQUARES

How about another puzzle involving squares? Your friends will need pencils and paper for this one.

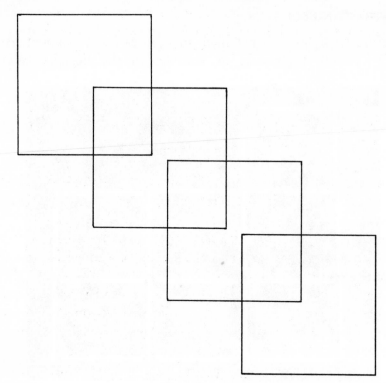

Four Squares

After drawing four interlocking squares, announce that everyone is to become an artist and copy those squares.

But:

The squares must be drawn in one continuous line. And no player may cross any line that has been drawn.

FRIENDS TOGETHER

To start this puzzle, you'll need to collect four pennies and four nickels from your audience. Arrange the coins in a row, with a nickel placed between each two adjacent pennies and a penny between each two adjacent nickels.

Now a player must rearrange the coins so that all the pennies are together and all the nickels are together. The coins must be moved two at a time. Only coins that are side by side may be moved. There must be no spaces between any two neighboring coins when the rearrangement is complete. *And* the whole job must be done in exactly *four* moves.

THREE COINS UP

While you've got coins on the table, you might want to use this puzzle as a follow-up to *Friends Together*.

Place three of the nickels in a row, with the middle one heads up, and the end ones tails up. A player is to turn them all heads up in exactly *three* moves. On each move, the player must pick up and turn over any two of the coins.

Be sure to insist that exactly three moves be taken. Otherwise, an alert player can end the fun in one move by simply turning over the two end coins.

Drinking glasses or matchboxes can be used for the puzzle in place of coins. In fact, any items with distinct tops and bottoms will work well. Some people are especially confused when three sets of reading glasses are placed in a row, with the nose bridge of one up and the bridges of the others down. The configuration of the reading glasses seems to keep the players from seeing (no pun intended!) the simple solution.

You can vary the puzzle a bit—and perhaps add to the fun —by quickly showing a player the three moves and then challenging him to repeat them. If your hands move swiftly and if you keep up a line of patter at the same time, the player will never remember exactly what you've done.

HEADS UP

Here is one of the most challenging of the world's many coin puzzles. It starts very innocently, when you place eight coins in a circle. They're all placed face down.

The object of the puzzle is to turn all the coins face up, except one. This sounds pretty easy until you tell the player the rules that must be followed. He may begin anywhere in the circle, but he must count off four coins in a clockwise direction. He is to turn the fourth coin face up. Again, starting anywhere that he wishes, he is to count off another four coins and turn the fourth one face up. He is to continue working in the same fashion until all but one coin have their heads up.

Now for the difficult part: He must always *begin* his count on a coin that is face down, and he must, of course, end every count on a coin that is face down.

Try it for yourself. Until you figure out the solution, you'll always be in trouble by the fourth or fifth move.

SQUARE THE MATCHES

Square the Matches is one of the simplest and most famous of puzzles. It is easily over a hundred years old. Yet it has the power to stump the brightest of people.

Exactly as is shown, place four matches in the form of a cross. A player is now to form a perfect square with the matches by moving just *one* match.

One hint: Because this puzzle is so famous, many teenagers and adults probably know its solution. And so you may

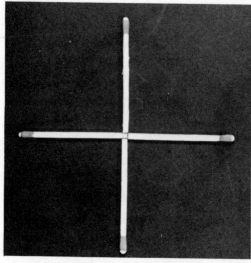

Square the Matches Setup

be wise to save it for those times when you're performing for small children. Old though it is, it will be something new and delightful for them.

FOUR TO FIVE

This puzzle is also especially suitable for small children. They'll be charmed and amused by its solution—and gleeful if they can see the solution for themselves.

Hold up a square sheet of paper and a pair of scissors. Point out the four corners of the sheet and then ask:

"Can you give this paper five corners by making just *one* cut with the scissors?"

THE TWO-CUT SQUARE

Here's a puzzler that's similar to *Four to Five*, but somewhat more difficult. It's suitable for both children and adults.

Cut out a sheet of paper in the shape pictured, and pencil it into five squares. Then hand a pair of scissors to a friend and ask him to cut the paper into three pieces that, when joined together, will form a square. He is to make only two, straight cuts.

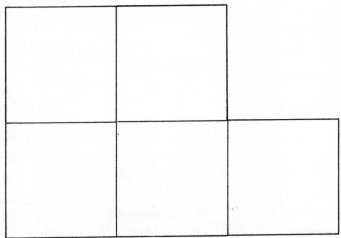

The Two-cut Square Setup

CHECKERBOARD FRUSTRATION

Now, for a last puzzle, here's still another one that's equally good for children and adults.

You'll need eight checkers and a checkerboard. All then that someone must do is arrange the checkers on the board in such a way that no two will be in the same line, either horizontally, vertically, or diagonally.

Few friends will balk at the challenge, for the puzzle seems so simple at first glance. But practically every player will spend long minutes finding the solution—and some will never come upon it.

When you try it for the first time, check the clock as you begin. You'll be surprised how long you'll be knitting your brows over this stumper.

Games

The first two games in this section are "card races." Several players are each given a number of cards and challenged to solve a problem with them. The first to do so, of course, is declared the winner.

Once again, so that you can have the fun of solving the problems for yourself, the answers are being withheld until the end of the chapter.

Ready? Here we go.

THE HOURGLASS RACE

Each player is given seven cards that run from the *two* through the *eight*. The cards are placed in the hourglass arrangement shown. They should be placed face up and in no particular numerical order. Then the players are to imagine that invisible lines run among the cards, forming them into vertical, horizontal, and diagonal lines of three cards each.

On the signal "go," the cards in each player's hourglass are

Hourglass Race Setup

to be rearranged—but rearranged so that their spots total 15 in each three-card row.

If the players would like to race again after the first game, give them another seven cards, this time running from the *ace* through *seven;* the ace counts as 1 and the total for each three-card row becomes 12. For a third race, use cards ranging from *three* through *nine,* and a total of 18 per line.

THE TWENTY-ONE CLOCK

For those players who still want to go on racing, here's a similar but somewhat more challenging game.

Each player receives a full suit of cards, from the *ace*

Twenty-one Clock Setup

through the *king*—thirteen cards in all. The cards are arranged, face up, in a clock-face pattern with one card placed
in the middle. Again, the cards should not be placed in any
special numerical order. And again, the players should imagine that lines divide the pattern into three-card rows.

For counting purposes, the ace is *1*; the jack is *11*, the queen, 12, and the king, 13. As usual, spot cards are counted at face value.

The race: Be the first to rearrange the cards so that each three-card row totals 21.

If you'd like to make the game a bit more difficult, keep the exact total from the players. Instead, tell them that there is only one total that will work for all the rows and that it is somewhere between 18 and 23. Then let them find it for themselves.

LAST-CARD CHALLENGE ✵ 1

This game, which is probably as old as card playing itself, begins when you lay out fifteen cards, face down, in a row. You and a friend then take turns picking up cards. Without fail, you force your opponent to pick up the last card.

The game has just two rules. The players must take alternate turns. Each player must pick up from *one* to *three* cards during each turn.

How can you be sure to win every time?

There is no puzzle here for you to solve and so there's no need to withhold the answer to the end of the chapter. You'll always win if, at one point in the game, you leave *five cards on the table*. Then, depending on what your opponent does next, you end the game with one of the following moves. Each leaves the last card behind.

1. If your opponent takes one card, you pick up three.
2. If your opponent takes two, pick up two.
3. If your opponent takes three, pick up one.

And that's all there is to it.

Your win will be automatic right from the start if you take the first turn. Just be sure to pick up two cards, leaving thirteen behind. Then immediately put the above formula of moves to use. It will leave nine cards on the table. Now apply the formula again. Five cards will be left behind.

There is an element of risk for you if your opponent takes the first turn. But the odds of a win are still all in your favor, for you have two chances to put the formula to work. First, try to arrange your moves so that you leave nine cards on the table; from then on, you can use the formula for a win. Second, should you be unable to leave nine cards for your opponent, you still have the chance to leave him with five.

LAST-CARD CHALLENGE ✳2

Last-card Challenge can be turned around so that the player who picks up the last card is the winner. To the frustration of your opponent, that last card always goes to you.

Thirty cards are now set out, face down. The players take alternate turns picking up cards. This time, however, each player must pick up between *one* and *six* cards per turn.

You are certain of a win if you pick up any of three cards during the course of the game: the ninth card, the thirteenth card, or the twenty-third card. Best of all, you should pick up all three of them.

Let's see how each of them insures a win.

Suppose that you pick up the twenty-third card. Left in the game are seven cards. No matter what your opponent does, you'll be able to gather in the last card on your next play. If he takes just one, you'll be able to pick up a full quota of six for the win. If he takes two, you win by taking the remaining five—and so on.

Now for the ninth and thirteenth cards: If you can take one or both, you'll be able to arrange your moves so that, no matter the number of cards taken by your opponent, you'll be the one to pick up the twenty-third card. You'll see how this never fails to work, if you practice the game a few times by yourself.

The ninth card is all-important. When you pick it up, you will win the game automatically. All that you need to do is follow a simple formula: be sure that the number of cards that you pick up on any following turn always totals *seven* when added to the number just taken by your opponent. Try a few practice hands to prove it to yourself.

You'll also win automatically if you take the first turn. Pick up just two cards. No matter the number then taken by your opponent, you'll be able to grab the ninth card on the next play. Should your opponent go first, keep your eye on the key cards and try to take them for yourself.

Solutions to Puzzles and Card Races

Here now are the solutions to the ten puzzles and the two card races. Let's see how well you did.

CARDS CROSS

Simply remove the card from the bottom of the vertical row and place it on top of the card that is at the juncture of the two rows in the cross. Each row now contains four cards.

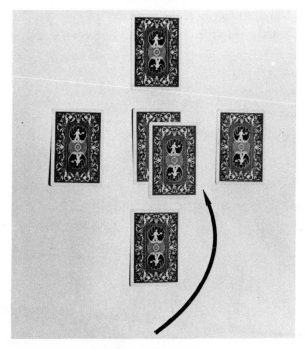

Cards Cross Solution

TWO-BY-FOUR

There they are—two squares and four triangles. Nothing more needs to be said.

Two-by-Four Solution

TURN-AROUND TRIANGLE

Remember, the puzzle is to be solved in three moves:

Move 1: Card 7 to the left of Card 2
Move 2: Card 10 to the right of Card 3.
Move 3: Card 1 down to below and between Cards 8 and 9.

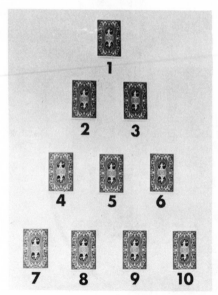

Turn-Around Triangle Solution

SUBTRACTING SQUARES

Only three matches need to be moved. Just shift them to the positions shown.

Subtracting Squares Solution

FOUR SQUARES

This puzzle is actually easier to solve than it first appears to be. Just draw the squares following the numbered lines.

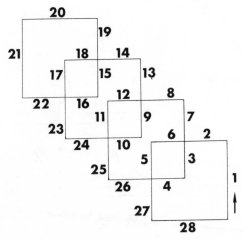

Four Squares Solution

FRIENDS TOGETHER

Begin by assigning the numbers 1 through 8 to the coins, and the numbers 9 and 10 to the open spaces to the right. Then:

Move 1: Move coins 2 and 3 to spaces 9 and 10. Spaces 2 and 3 are now open.

Move 2: Move coins 5 and 6 to spaces 2 and 3. Spaces 5 and 6 are now open.

Move 3: Move coins 8 and 9 to spaces 5 and 6. Spaces 8 and 9 are now open.

Move 4: Move coins 1 and 2 to spaces 8 and 9. All the "friends" are together now.

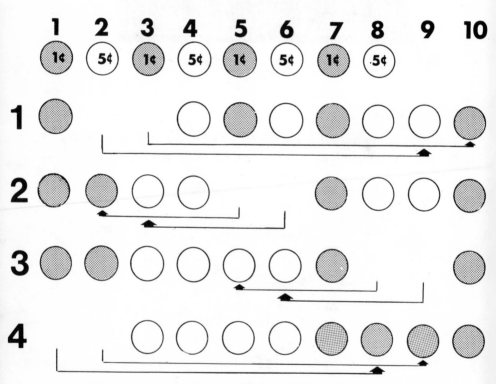

Friends Together Solution

THREE COINS UP

Again, assign numbers to the coins—from *1* to *3*. Then:

Move 1: Turn over coins 2 and 3.
Move 2: Turn over coins *1* and 3.
Move 3: Turn over coins 2 and 3. All coins are now showing heads.

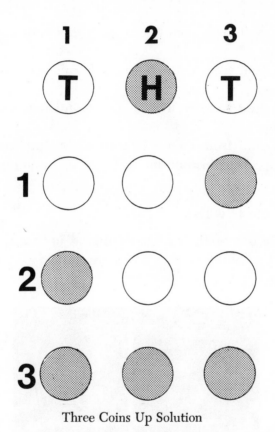

Three Coins Up Solution

HEADS UP

As you know, you may begin to count the coins from any point in the circle. From your starting point, number the coins from 1 through 8 in a clockwise direction. Then, always counting clockwise, try the following moves:

Move 1: Count from coin *1* to coin *4* and turn coin *4* heads up.

Move 2: Count from coin *6* to coin *1* and turn coin *1* heads up.

Move 3: Count from coin *3* to coin *6* and turn coin *6* heads up.

Move 4: Count from coin *8* to coin *3* and turn coin *3* heads up.

Move 5: Count from coin *5* to coin *8* and turn coin *8* heads up.

Move 6: Count from coin *2* to coin *5* and turn coin *5* heads up.

Move 7: Count from coin *7* to coin *2* and turn coin *2* heads up. All coins but one will now be turned heads up.

SQUARE THE MATCHES

Just move one of the matches outward until a square forms at the point where the match bases are formed.

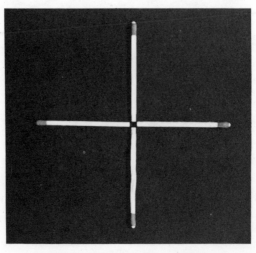

Square the Matches Solution

FOUR TO FIVE

Four to Five Solution

THE TWO-CUT SQUARE

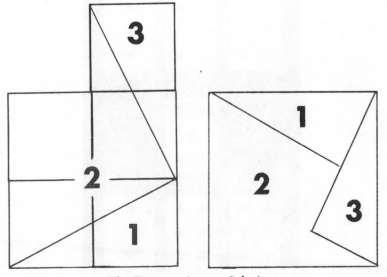

The Two-cut Square Solution

CHECKERBOARD FRUSTRATION

Checkerboard Frustration Solution

THE HOURGLASS RACE

The Hourglass Race Solution

THE TWENTY-ONE CLOCK

The Twenty-one Clock Solution

4

More Card Magic

In this chapter, we turn to a more advanced card magic—in fact, to two different kinds of card magic. First, we'll look at what is called *key card* trickery. Then we'll try some little mysteries that call for you to develop three new skills in the handling of the deck.

Ready? Curtain up.

Key-card Magic

As was said when you were practicing the shuffle, in Chapter 3, many a trick requires you to know the top or bottom card in the deck. Either can be sighted and memorized at a glance if you are able to shuffle with ease. Or either may be glimpsed as you handle the deck before asking someone to take a card. As soon as either is known to you, it becomes your *key card* in the trick.

Quite simply, a key card is one that enables you to locate the card chosen by a member of the audience. The chosen card is unknown to you, but you're always able to find it, because you've secretly arranged to have it placed next to your key card. For instance:

Suppose that the bottom card is the *queen of spades* (Picture *A*). After a friend takes a card, you instruct him to place it on top of the deck (Picture *B*). You now cut the

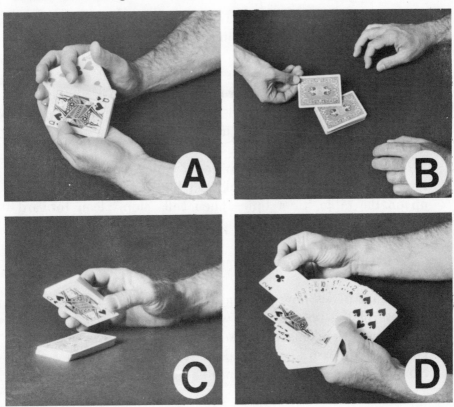

The Key Card

cards (Picture C) and bring your queen into a position directly above the chosen card. To produce the chosen card (Picture D), just pull out the one to the right of your key card. This has to be your friend's card because, were the deck still flat on the table, it would be the one directly beneath the queen.

Basically, that's all there is to it. So let's put the key card to work. As we go along, we'll add a few little wrinkles to befuddle the audience even more.

THIS IS YOUR CARD

To begin, here is one of the oldest and simplest of the key-card tricks. But it can be made to look especially mystifying.

Just don't touch the cards again after you've shuffled them at the start. Let the audience think that you're performing your magic at a distance.

Once you've shuffled, place the deck in front of a friend and ask him to take a card from it. He is to look at the card without letting you see it and is to place it face down on top of the deck. Then he is to cut the deck, setting the bottom half on top of the upper half.

Now instruct your friend to begin removing cards one at a time from the top of the deck. Let him drop each card face up on the table for a time. Then call "stop," lean forward, point to the card now at the top of the deck, and announce:

"This is your card."

Your words, of course, come true when he turns the card up.

It's easy to see how this one works. As you shuffle, catch a glimpse of the bottom card—we'll say it's the *jack of hearts*. Once your friend makes his selection and cuts the deck, you know that his card is lying directly beneath your key card. Now all you need do is wait until he turns the jack up.

FOLLOW THE LEADER

Though a simple trick, *Follow the Leader* always startles audiences. After a series of seemingly complicated moves, you produce the card that was selected by a spectator.

Shuffle the deck and ask a friend to cut it into two equal packets. Have him take the packet that was the bottom half of the deck. He holds it face down in his hands while you hold the other packet in the same way. Now he is to play "follow the leader," duplicating your every move.

First move: Draw a card from somewhere near the center of your packet and, keeping it face down, place it on top of the packet. Your friend does the same. But before he places the card on top of the packet, have him look at it and memorize it. He is not to show it to you. Let's say that he chooses the *four of diamonds*.

Second move: Remove the top half of your packet and place it on the bottom. Your friend follows suit.

Third move: Hand your packet to your friend. Take his in return.

Fourth move: Once you've exchanged packets, fan the cards (keeping their backs to your friend), select a card and place it face down on the table. As your friend duplicates your moves, ask him to remember the new card as well as the one he selected a moment ago.

At this point, you each have a card face down on the table. Now it's time for you to ask some questions.

"Do you remember the first card you took from your packet?"

"Yes."

"The card that you've just put on the table—is it higher or lower than that first card?"

Let's say that your friend answers, "Higher."

"How much higher?"

And let's say that he replies, "Two."

"Good! The card that you just put on the table is a *six*. Because the first card you looked at was . . ."

With a dramatic movement, flip over the card that you put on the table.

"The four of diamonds! Right?"

He'll only be able to stare at you and mutter, "Right" or "How'd you do that?"

The answer to his question goes back to the start of the trick. While shuffling or handling the deck, learn your key card. It's the one at the bottom. In this instance, we'll suppose that it's the *king of clubs*.

Next, when your friend cuts the cards, he is instructed to hold the packet that was the lower half of the deck. You know that your king is at the bottom of that packet.

Now, imitating you, he takes a card, looks at it, and places it on top of his packet. Then he removes the top half of the packet and places it beneath the lower half. This movement places his selected card directly beneath the king.

Next, after the exchange of packets, your friend fans the cards, picks one at random, memorizes it, and places it face down on the table. For your part, you seem to be selecting a card at random, but actually you're looking for your key king. To its immediate right is the four of diamonds. Remove the four and place it face down on the table.

As far as you're concerned, your work is done. The questions that you now ask your friend are meant to add a little drama and mystery to the end of the trick.

Incidentally, because you do ask your friend to add or subtract at the end of the trick, you should set number values for the ace and face cards in case he picks one of them. Value the ace as *1;* the jack as *11;* the queen, *12;* and the king, *13.*

CARD POINTER ※1

In the preceding tricks, the bottom card served as your key card. *Card Pointer* ※*1* is a bit fancier. It uses *two* key cards.

During the shuffle, memorize both the top and the bottom cards; in this case, let's suppose they're the *seven of hearts* at the bottom and the *jack of clubs* at the top (Picture A). Spread the cards out in a face-down fan (Picture B) and have a friend select one. After secretly noting the card, he is to place it at one end of the fan or the other (Picture C). It makes no difference at which end the card is placed.

Ask him now to close the fan and cut the deck. He may cut as often as he wishes. Each cut should be a single one, with the divided deck being rejoined before the next cut.

When he has finished cutting, have him spread the cards in a broad fan just as you did earlier. This time, however, the cards are to be spread face up.

Now sweep your hand back and forth above the fan. Add to the drama by murmuring a few magic phrases. Then let your hand drop to the fan. Pick out your friend's card and hand it to him.

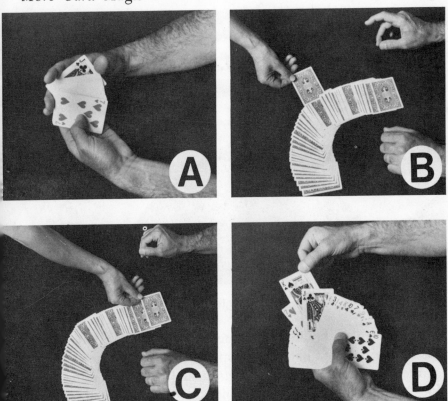

Card Pointer #1

In this instance, the selected card is the *king of spades* (Picture *D*). It's easily sighted lying between your *seven* and *jack*, having been put there when the deck was cut for the first time. The several cuts that followed did nothing to disturb the placement of the three cards.

CARD POINTER #2

This is a very simple variation of *Card Pointer* #1. It is performed in much the same way, except that you have your friend select two cards instead of one.

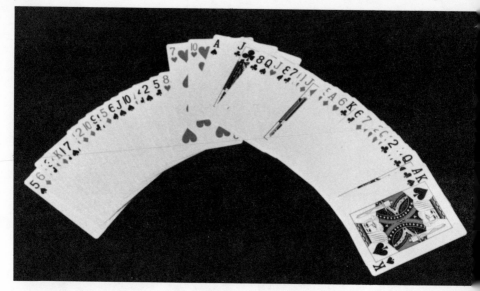

Card Pointer #2

Again, when shuffling, glimpse the top and bottom cards; for ease of explanation, let's keep them as the *seven of hearts* at the bottom and the *jack of clubs* at the top. Fan the deck face down, ask your friend to pick two cards, and then have him place one at the top of the deck and the other at the bottom. Let him close the fan and cut the deck as often as he pleases. As before, each cut should be a single one.

Now take the cards in hand and fan them in front of you, keeping their backs to the audience. As shown, you'll find your friend's cards—in this instance, the *ace of spades* and the *ten of hearts*—sandwiched between your key cards. Pass one hand back and forth in front of the cards, pause, remove the ace, and place it at the top of the deck. Sweep your hand over the fan again, remove the ten, and place it at the bottom.

Close the fan and turn the deck face down in one hand. Ask your friend to name his cards one at a time. Should he call the ten first, take it from the bottom of the deck and drop it face up in front of him. On his next call, pull the ace from the top.

Just one caution: When removing the selected cards from

the fan, never forget to take them one at a time. Let your hand move back and forth along the fan for a few seconds between the first and second removals. This keeps the audience from seeing that both cards are being taken from the very same spot in the deck. If you wish, you may conceal the movement of your friend's cards by shifting several other cards to new positions at the same time.

Handling the Cards

Now that you've had some practice working with key cards, it's time to add three more skills to your "bag of tricks." They are the *force,* the *pass,* and the *false shuffle.* The first two open the way to new tricks, and the third adds to the mystery of your performance.

Just as the key card does, the force enables you to identify a friend's card. However, you now identify the chosen card *before* your friend takes it. Then, magician that you are, you maneuver him—force him—into picking that very card. He thinks he's selecting a card at random. But you know better.

Professional magicians use complicated force methods that require much practice to master. Here, though, is a simple one that you can put to use right away.

Note and memorize the bottom card—let's say it's the *ace of spades*—as you shuffle. Place the deck on the table and have your friend cut it. Instruct him to complete the cut (Picture A) by placing the bottom half on top of the upper half but at right angles to it. Then ask him to pick up what is now the top half of the deck (Picture B) and look at its bottom card. You've forced him into selecting the card that you've already identified. You're now ready to proceed with your trickery and "miraculously" pick out that card, no matter where it is hidden in the deck.

You can vary the force by noting the *top* card as you shuffle. Your friend cuts the deck exactly as before. He sets the lower half on top of the upper half and places them at right angles to each other.

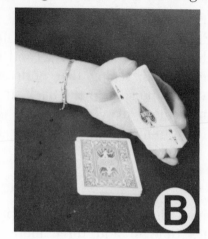

The Force—Bottom Card

You lift away what is now the top half and ask your friend to look at the first card on the bottom half. Again, you've forced him to select the card that you want him to take. And he'll think it's magic when you pick out that card later in the trick.

It's a good idea to master both the key-card and the force methods. They can be used interchangeably in many tricks and so can give variety to your performance; you'll reduce the risk of having the audience "see through" one trick because you began it in the same way as another. Also, there are many tricks—we'll be trying some in a moment—that can be worked only with the force.

Quite often, once you've forced a card on a friend, you'll need to bring it to the top of the deck before you can complete the trick. The movement, of course, must be a secret one. It is accomplished by means of the pass. If done smoothly, the pass can be made with the audience right on top of you—and no one will be the wiser.

Following the pictures, let's see how it works.

Once the deck is cut into two right-angled packets, open the way to the pass by forcing your friend to take the top card on the lower packet. As he is looking at the card (Picture *A*), place the lower packet face down in your left hand and hold the upper packet nearby in your right hand. Next (Picture *B*), have your friend place his card on the packet in your left hand.

As he is doing so, pay close attention to the fingers of your left hand (Picture *B*). Your middle, ring, and little fingers should be spaced along the side of the cards, with the little finger right at the lower corner. Be sure that the little finger is positioned correctly. It's the most important one of the lot.

Once the selected card is in place, bring the packet in your right hand over and place it on top of the left one. But, as you do so (Picture *C*), bend your little finger over the left packet so that there is a break between the two packets.

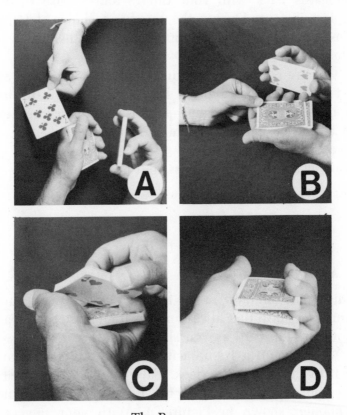

The Pass

If you now hold the deck tilted slightly upward at the front (Picture *D*), the break will be hidden from the audience. Complete the cut by drawing the bottom packet out and placing it on the top packet. The forced card is now at the top of the deck.

Once the forced card is in place, you may want to shuffle the deck. An extra shuffle after someone has picked a card always convinces your viewers that you can't possibly know where it is. But you want to leave the forced card right there at the top of the deck. And so out comes the false shuffle.

You may false-shuffle with either the riffle or the overhand shuffle. All that you do in either case is make sure to leave the same three or four cards at the top of the deck, with the forced card resting safely on them. When riffle-shuffling, hold these cards back with your thumb and release them in the very last instant. During the overhand shuffle, let them rest against your fingers while you pull away other cards in small clusters.

If you are able to shuffle quickly and easily, your audience won't be aware that you're holding the top card in place. You can further hide your actions by distracting everyone with a line of patter. The false shuffle can also be used to keep a bottom card in place.

Now let's put the force, pass, and false shuffle to use.

From Force to False Shuffle

THE ASCENDING CARD

This is the simplest of all force-and-pass tricks. But it has an amusing finish that always makes it an audience pleaser.

Note the top card as you shuffle: the *five of spades* in this case. Force it on a friend with the right-angle cut and then pass it to the top of the deck. False-shuffle if you wish. Now, using your right hand, hold the deck up to the audience in the manner shown in Picture *A* With your fingers to the

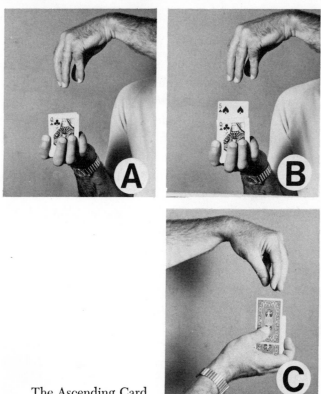

The Ascending Card

front of the cards and your thumb to the rear, you're ready for the "big finish."

Concentrate for a moment and dramatically announce, "Your card is the five of spades." In the same instant, bring your left hand above the deck, with your fingers pointing downward. Move the hand up and down. Miraculously, as if drawn by invisible strings attached to your fingers, the chosen card rises slowly from the deck (Picture *B*).

Invisible strings have nothing to do with this bit of magic. The concealed thumb of your right hand does the work (Picture *C*). It gently pushes the card upward. If you wish, you can position the little finger of your left hand so that it touches the upper edge of the card and helps to guide it straight up from the deck.

SPELL YOUR NAME

There is no force card in this trick. All the magic depends on the pass. Just follow the steps below and that magic will work automatically every time.

Have a friend pick a card at random. While he is looking at his choice, divide the deck into two packets and hold them in your hands. Ask your friend to place his card on top of the left packet. Bring the packets together, with the right one on top of the left. Pass the left packet to the top. If you wish, false-shuffle.

Your friend is now to spell his name aloud. Let's say that it's *Bill Royse*. As he calls out each letter, place a card face down on the table. But pause on the final *e*. Ask your friend to name his card.

Suppose he answers, "The ace of clubs."

Deal out the card triumphantly, dropping it face up. "There it is!"

But there's something wrong. It's not the ace. Look puzzled for a moment. Then say, "Of course. I forgot. I'm not supposed to deal the cards in this trick. You are."

Quickly gather up the nine cards that have been dealt, putting the *e* card on top. Hand the deck to your friend. Let him now toss out a card at a time as he spells his name. Tell him to flip over the final card. It will be the ace of clubs.

The ace was at the top of the deck when your friend initially spelled his name and so it was the first card to be dealt onto the table. Then, when you gathered up the dealt cards after seeming to bungle things, it was at the bottom of the nine-card pile. It can't help now but show itself on the last letter when the name is spelled again.

THE SHOVEL TRICK

Again, you need not know the identity of the chosen card. But you do need a pair of sharp eyes to work the amusing *Shovel Trick*.

Start by passing your friend's card to the top of the deck.

False-shuffle if you want to add a bit more mystery. Then set the cards out in three heaps. Next, divide the three heaps into six. Don't set the heaps in a neat row. Rather, place them at random about the table.

Once the heaps are placed, draw a card face down from the top of one of them. Explain that you're going to use it as a shovel to turn over the chosen card. Insert the shovel card into one of the heaps and ask your friend, "Are you ready to see your card?" Flip over the heap with your shovel card.

"Is that your card? No? Well, I'm not surprised. Because—" With that, turn the shovel card face up.

"Here it is!"

Once the chosen card is passed to the top of the deck, you have only one real job left in this trick. While dividing the cards into heaps, just keep track of the heap with the chosen card at its top. Then you'll know exactly where to go for your "shovel."

In addition to setting out the heaps at random, you should work quickly and cover your actions with a line of patter. All this will keep the audience from seeing that you take the shovel card from the heap that had been at the top of the deck. No one's suspicions will be aroused.

THE CHANGE-OF-COLOR ACE

All the tricks thus far have needed no preparation. They can be done at any time and with your own or borrowed cards. Now, to end the chapter, here's one of a different sort. The deck needs to be prepared ahead of time.

Before talking about the preparation, let's watch the trick and see how it looks. It begins when you hold the deck in your right hand (Picture A) and riffle the cards with your left to show that they all have red backs. Next (Picture B), a friend takes a card—it's the *ace of spades*—and returns it to the deck. You riffle the cards again, once more showing them all to be red-backed. But when they are spread out in a face-down fan (Picture C, there among them is a card with a *blue*

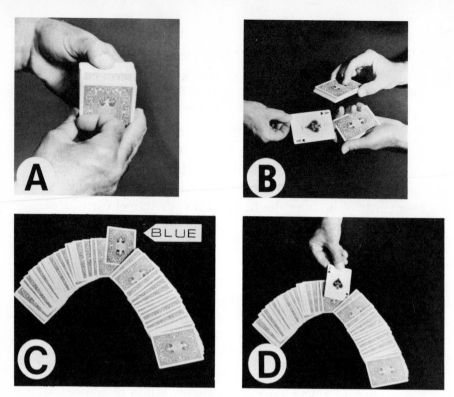

The Change-of-color Ace

back. On being turned over (Picture D), it proves to be your friend's ace.

How's the trick done?

First, you need two aces of spades—one with a red back and one from a blue-backed deck of identical design. Carefully cut off both ends of the blue ace to make it about ⅜ inch shorter than the red ace. To get the straightest cut possible, use a razor blade or an X-acto knife, and a ruler as a guide. Avoid scissors; they're too likely to cut in a wavy line. Don't forget to round off the corners.

Second, place the blue ace in the middle of the red deck and push it down until its lower edge is flush with the lower edge of the deck. It will not be seen when you riffle the cards. Being shorter than the others, it will be caught and carried forward, unnoticed, by the cards behind it. Try riffling the cards a few times. Even though you're looking for it, the ace will remain hidden.

Finally, place the red-backed ace at the top or bottom of the deck so that you can force it on your friend.

The Change-of-color Ace, of course, cannot be repeated. And it should be worked at a good speed. As soon as the blue-backed ace is sighted in the face-down fan, draw it out; don't give the audience time to see that it's shorter than the other cards. For the same reason, don't hand it to your friend, but just show it around the table. Then remove the deck so that no one can pick it up and discover that there's a red-backed ace of spades in it.

Performing Tips

1. It's a good idea to work in front of a mirror when practicing the pass and the false shuffle. Your reflection will let you see how you appear to the audience. You'll be able to catch and correct any mistakes that can be easily seen from their viewpoint.

2. Practice diligently, working for the day when—no matter how closely you're watching yourself in the mirror—you can actually fool yourself.

3. When not practicing, get into the habit of just handling the cards. Cut, fan, shuffle, and deal them. They'll soon feel very comfortable in your hands and you'll find yourself manipulating them with an increasing ease and smoothness.

4. Develop a line of patter to go along with your passes and false shuffles, especially the false shuffles. An alert audience will always be watching your hands. A bit of patter is a nice distraction. But just a bit. Remember, too much talk can smother a trick.

5. Keep a few little jokes or amusing sayings on tap for use should something go wrong. Don't be embarrassed or flustered if a trick fails. Poke a bit of fun at yourself, and if it can be restarted easily, try the trick again. Otherwise, move right on to your next routine.

5

Stunt Magic

A stunt is some little feat of physical or mental prowess that seems impossible to perform. And impossible it is unless you know its "catch"—the secret and simple way of doing it.

THE IMPOSSIBLE CARD

Drop a playing card flat on a table and dare a friend to blow under the card so that it flips over on its back. After pressing his cheek against the table and puffing a few times, he'll have to give up. But if you know the "catch," you can do the impossible. Just move the card until about half of it hangs over the edge of the table. Crouch beneath the card. One upward burst of breath does the rest.

The catches behind stunts are not only simple but also obvious. But even the smartest of people never seem to think of them when challenged to try the "impossible." On being revealed, the catches usually draw a laugh and a few groans of "So that's it!"

Stunts are fine companions for puzzles and games at parties. They're all amusing, and most are audience-participation tricks. The guests, rather than just watching you perform as a magician, have a chance to take an active part in the fun.

Here now are twelve stunts. We'll start with those that call for your friends to try some impossible physical task. Then we'll turn to those that will prove you—and anyone who can guess the catches—a mental wizard.

Physical Stunts

THE BALANCED CARD

Let's start with the playing card that your friend couldn't blow over. Drop it on the table again, but this time challenge everyone to take turns trying to balance it on its edge.

Let frustration reign for a few moments. Then announce that you can do the job in less than five seconds. Dare someone to time you.

To beat the time limit, bend the card into a shallow curve by placing it flat in your palm and then closing your hand slightly. The stiffness of the card will hold the curve long enough for the card to be balanced on edge.

CARD TARGET PRACTICE

To begin this stunt, put the bent card aside and hand a friend the rest of the deck from which it was taken. Have him stand beside a hat that you've placed upside down on the floor.

Your challenge is a simple one: One by one, he is to drop as many cards as he wishes into the hat from waist height. When he's done, you'll drop the same number of cards, one at a time, from the same height. You'll succeed in getting more cards into the hat than he does.

Unless your friend knows the catch, you'll always win.

Your friend will undoubtedly hold each of his cards by a corner between his thumb and forefinger. When dropped, the cards will flutter as they fall, with most of them finally landing alongside the hat. You'll win the game by holding each card horizontally between your thumb and fingers before the release. They'll all drop straight toward the hat target.

CARD DEFYING GRAVITY

There are numerous card stunts, but many magicians feel that this one is the most startling of all.

Give a playing card to a friend and challenge him to press it against a wall in such a way that it stays there when he removes his hand. He may try—and of course, fail. Or he may refuse the dare, saying that you're asking the impossible.

It's of no matter what he does. In either case, take the card, slap it into place, and stroll away. There it will remain, stuck to the wall in defiance of all gravity.

Your friend will probably want to check the card, certain that you've attached a bit of wax or some other sticky substance to it. But there's not a thing to be seen—because static electricity is the "sticky substance."

Let's face one fact: This is a risky stunt and can fail if tried under the wrong conditions. It's best done in cold weather and when you're wearing leather-soled shoes. Scrape your feet on the rug while your friend is trying to put the card into place. Then, when you take the card, continue to scrape your feet as you walk to the wall. You'll build up enough static electricity to enable the card to "defy gravity."

THE BALANCING GLASS

Money interests people of all ages. So if you want to get everyone's attention quickly, place a dollar bill and a drinking glass side by side on a table. Then tell a friend that you'll give him the dollar bill if he can set it on its edge and then balance a drinking glass on top of it.

It just can't be done—not unless you know the "catch." Fold the bill into a small accordion of five equal sections. Then stand the bill on edge and gently place the glass on top of the center sections. A new—or fairly new—bill should be used; it will best support the weight of the glass.

You run only one risk with this stunt. You'll lose your money to anyone who already knows the catch. So be careful which friend you choose.

THE STEADY BOTTLE

The dollar bill can now be used for one of the oldest but most perplexing of stunts.

Place the bill flat on the table and set a soft-drink bottle upside down on it. Your friends are to take turns trying to remove the bill from beneath the bottle *without once touching or upsetting the bottle.*

How is it done? Someone is sure to try snatching the bill away in imitation of the magician who pulls a tablecloth from beneath a dinner setting without disturbing a single dish. But that's not the answer at all.

Rather, roll the bill up tightly from one end until it touches the bottle. Then, as you continue to roll the dollar, it will push the bottle along until the bottle comes free and stands alone. Work carefully so that the bottle doesn't fall. And keep your fingers out at the edges of the bill so that they never touch the bottle.

Incidentally, *The Steady Bottle* is best done on a bare table. A tablecloth too often snags the bill or begins to wrinkle under it, causing the bottle to fall. If you don't have a bare table, the stunt can be worked just as well on a magazine or a large book.

TWO STEADY BOTTLES

Want to make life a bit more difficult—and a bit more exciting—for your friends?

As shown, place the dollar bill between *two* bottles standing one atop the other. Then challenge them to remove the bill without touching or knocking either bottle over.

This stunt *is* quite similar to the one in which the magician pulls the tablecloth from under a dinner setting. Take the edge of the bill between the thumb and forefinger of one hand. Then strike the bill sharply with the extended forefinger of your other hand. Out will slide the bill, leaving the bottles untouched and standing.

Two Steady Bottles

THE COIN IN THE MIDDLE

Let's try a money stunt that uses coins instead of a dollar bill. Announcing that here's a chance to make some money, place a nickel on the table and set two pennies side by side about two inches away (Picture A). The pennies should not only be side by side but touching as well. Tell a friend that if he can place the nickel between the two pennies, he can keep it.

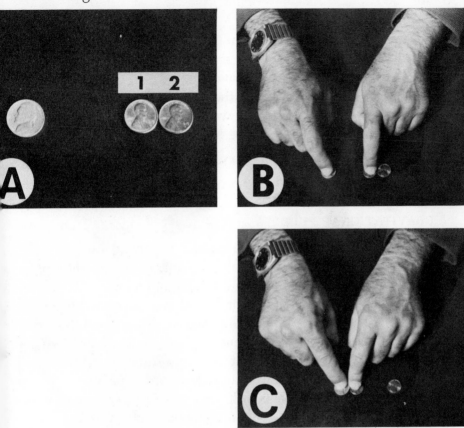

The Coin in the Middle

However, he may not touch penny 2 and he may not move penny 1.

Pictures B and C show the "catch" that makes this "impossible" stunt possible. Place the index finger of one hand firmly on penny 1 (this one can't be moved, but you didn't say that it couldn't be touched). Now, with the index finger of your other hand, slide the nickel along until it strikes penny 1. Penny 1 is held in place, but the force of the blow sends penny 2 skittering away. All that you do now is drop the nickel into the space left open between the two pennies.

THE INVISIBLE COIN

The catch behind this stunt is so simple as to be absurd. In fact, the friend that you try it on might never want to have anything to do with you again.

Hold up a nickel and give the friend ten seconds in which to place it on you in such a way that it will be *invisible to you but visible to everyone else* in the room.

When he runs out of time, take the nickel and deposit it on top of his head.

GRAVITATIONAL PULL

A few paragraphs ago, you caused a playing card to defy gravity. Now here's a stunt whose result is exactly the opposite. It's done with a quarter and a piece of paper.

You need to take a moment to cut the paper so that it is the same shape and size as the quarter. Then hand the coin and the paper to a friend and have him drop the two of them from the same height at the same time. Every time he tries, the coin, of course, will land ahead of the paper.

Throughout, insist that with your magic powers, you have the ability to equalize the gravitational pull. You can drop the coin and the paper and have them both strike the floor at the same time. You then very easily prove your point.

Balance the coin on your fingertip and place the paper on top of the coin. When you pull your finger away, the paper will "ride" the coin right down to the floor.

Mental Stunts

In the stunts above, you are forced to reveal the catches that make them work. The revealing is the main part of the fun. But it does pose a problem. It limits you to performing each stunt just once. As soon as the catch is revealed, the mystery is over.

There are stunts, however, in which the catches need not be revealed. They can be kept as much a secret as the methods used to perform your regular tricks. And so you are free to add to the fun and the mystery by repeating them several times while your friends try to figure out how they're worked.

Here now are three stunts with secret catches.

MAGIC CALCULATION

Magic Calculation begins when you tell your audience that you've discovered the secret of adding numbers with the speed of an electronic calculator. "Aha! I see that you don't believe me. I'll prove it to you. I'll add a column of figures that totals in the hundreds of thousands. And I'll do it at a glance."

Hand a sheet of paper and a pencil to three friends. Have the first friend jot down any five-figure number that comes to mind. The second friend writes a five-digit number directly under it. Now help matters along by quickly jotting down a five-digit number of your own. Then the third friend writes in a set of five numbers. Finish off by scribbling in another five figures of your own and drawing a line under them so that all the numbers can be added.

At this point, the sheet of paper may look like this:

15898—First friend's number
63124—Second friend's number
36875—Your number
46221—Third friend's number
53778—Your number

Because you are a human calculator, you wrote your two sets of numbers in very quickly (your speed will help your friends to think that you can't possibly be adding the numbers in your head as you go along). Now, just as quickly, glance at the sets of numbers, write a figure on a separate sheet of paper, and hand it to one of the three friends to hold. Next, have the friends total up the sets of numbers. Finally, ask them to open the separate sheet of paper.

The figure written there is 215896—the exact same total as that for the five sets of numbers. Your friends will have spent more than a minute reaching a total. But you'll have done it in a split second.

Well, you know that you're really not a human calculator. So how did you do it?

The whole stunt is based on a simple mathematical formula. The formula has three parts to it. The first part is hidden in the first set of figures that you scribbled on the sheet of paper.

15898—First friend's number
63124—Second friend's number
36875—Your number

Take a close look at your number and compare it with the second friend's number. See anything odd? Got it?

Right. You've jotted down figures that, when added to those of the second friend, all total 9.

63124—Second friend's number
36875—Your number
99999

Now, for the second part of the formula, check the five-digit number that you put below the number written by the third friend. Again, everything adds up to 9.

46221—Third friend's number
53778—Your final number
99999

By jotting down figures that always total 9 when added to the ones directly above, you mathematically pave the way to the third, and final, part of the formula. All you need do now is glance back to the five-digit number written by the first friend:

15898

And do no more than place a 2 in front of it, and subtract 2 from its last digit. You come up with:

215896

And that's all there is to being a "human calculator."

The formula always works, regardless of the numbers written by your friends. Try it yourself with various sets of five-digit numbers. You'll amaze yourself.

Beautiful, isn't it?

DATES TO REMEMBER

This trick is quite as baffling as *Magic Calculation*. And it is just as easy—if not easier—to perform.

Have a friend write four dates on a sheet of paper. The first is the year of his birth. The second is a year in which something important happened to him—perhaps the year he started high school, moved to his present home, or got his first job. The third is the number of years that have passed since the year of that important event. The fourth is his age as it will be at the end of the present year.

Ask him to finish everything off by adding up the four figures. If the trick is being performed in 1977, the column of figures may look like this:

    1955—Year of birth
    1969—Important year (start of high school)
       8—Years since important year
      22—Age at the end of the present year
    ————
    3954

As the friend writes down the figures and totals them, pay no attention to him. Rather, scribble a series of numbers on a sheet of paper, fold it, and set it to one side. When he completes his total, have him take your sheet of paper and open it. The numbers written on it will match exactly the total of his figures: 3954.

Again, you seem to have magic powers. But not really.

You've just worked another mathematical catch. All you've
done is multiply the year in which the trick is worked by 2.

$$1977 \times 2 = 3954$$

One caution, however: Since 1977 multiplied by 2 always
comes to the same total, you really shouldn't repeat the stunt,
because the audience will quickly see the light. If you do try
the stunt twice, be sure to pocket the totals reached by you
and your friend and then talk a bit to give the audience time
to forget them. Better yet, suggest that the audience pretend
the trick is being performed in some future or past year, such
as 1989 and 1965. You'll be protecting yourself, but they'll
think that you're showing your brilliance by making things
harder on yourself.

THE TIME TAP

The Time Tap can be performed with any sort of clock, or
with a set of numbers drawn as a clock face on a sheet of
paper. Place the clock on a table and instruct a friend to select an hour at random while your back is turned. With your
magical abilities, you'll be able to point to the chosen number.

Once the hour is selected, return to the table and explain
that you plan to tap the numbers on the clock at random.
Your friend is to keep track of the taps, but is to do so in a
special way. Let's say that the selected hour is five o'clock.
On your first tap, he is to count 6 to himself. He is then to
keep counting silently upward until he reaches 20, at which
time he is to call "stop." Your finger will be pointing to five
o'clock.

The same procedure is to be followed no matter the hour
chosen. Your friend is to begin his silent count at one number
above the secret hour—4 for three o'clock, 2 for one o'clock, and
so on—and is to continue counting from there to 20. You'll
always be touching the chosen hour on the twentieth count.

What's the secret?

For your first seven counts, tap various hours at random. But on the eighth count, be sure to tap twelve o'clock. Then, on each succeeding tap, move around the dial in a counterclockwise direction: going to eleven o'clock, ten, nine, eight, and so on. On the twentieth count, you'll be at the selected hour.

When you touch twelve o'clock, you have a certain number of hours between there and the selected hour. And when you touch twelve o'clock on the eighth tap, your friend has a certain number of counts left until he reaches the twentieth. The number of hours left in a counterclockwise direction always matches the number of counts left.

Here's how everything works with five o'clock as the selected hour: When your friend starts his count at 6, he is at 13 on your eighth tap. Seven counts are left until the twentieth. And seven hours separate twelve o'clock from five o'clock when you move in a counterclockwise direction.

Suppose that the secret hour is three o'clock. Your friend begins to count from 4. On your eighth tap, he reaches 11. Nine counts will take him to 20. Moving counterclockwise, nine hours will take you to three o'clock.

As clever as it is, *The Time Tap* contains a flaw that you must guard against on repeat performances. Your audience won't quickly see that you always touch twelve o'clock on your eighth tap. But they'll soon catch on that you always end the trick by counting steadily down through eleven o'clock, ten, nine, and so on.

A little practice will take care of the problem. Develop the knack of hopping about the face on the countdown from twelve o'clock. For instance, when you reach nine o'clock, you might tap it twice and then jump to seven o'clock. Or, when you should be touching eleven o'clock, you might jump over to one o'clock and then come back to ten o'clock.

6

String and Silk Magic

For many spectators, the tricks done with silk handkerchiefs and lengths of string are the most astonishing in magic. Wonders of every sort occur. String is cut and then restored to a single piece. Knots appear without the string or silk ever being tied. Handkerchiefs are knotted securely together, only to fly apart when tossed into the air. The magician is tightly bound, but escapes in a matter of seconds.

For the magician, the tricks are particular fun. Practically all are made possible by dexterous but simple hand movements. Once these movements are learned, the tricks become some of the easiest you'll ever perform. In fact, what is truly astonishing about string and silk magic is that such simple actions can produce such puzzling wonders.

So roll up your sleeves and flex your fingers. Here we go.

String Magic

THE MAGIC KNOT

The Magic Knot is a mainstay trick for every string magician. A spectator ties the ends of a string or cord about your wrists. Holding your wrists apart, you show the audience that there isn't a knot anywhere in the cord that now stretches

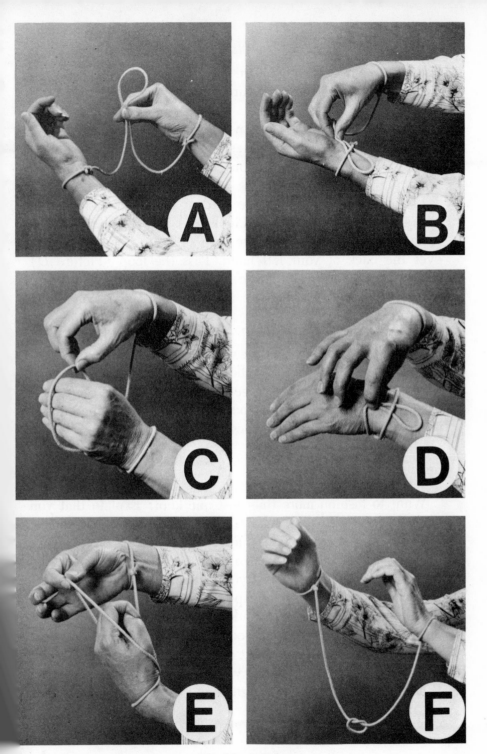

The Magic Knot

between them. Then you turn away. Less than five seconds later, you're facing front again—and displaying a knot midway along the cord.

Five seconds certainly doesn't give you the time to remove a cord end from one wrist, fashion the knot, and then retie the end to your wrist. But you can beat the five seconds by following the pictures:

First (Picture A), grasp the cord at its center and bend it into a loop. Insert the loop (Picture B) beneath the cord circling your left wrist. Twist the loop (Picture C) and carry it over the back of your left hand. Pass the loop (Picture D) under the cord. Now (Picture E) pull the loop forward and over your left fingers. Release the loop and there's your knot (Picture F).

The trick is best performed with a slim cord about fifteen to twenty inches long. The cord is easy to handle and the length allows you to form the knot without bringing your wrists uncomfortably close together. You may work with ordinary string, if you wish, but you'll run the risk of some tangles until you've perfected the moves.

THE MYSTERY LASSO

Want to fashion more than just one knot? Explain that you recently met a cowboy who could tie knots in his lasso just by wrapping it around his hand. Suit your actions to your words and then flick one end of the cord free. Knots will be spaced all along the length of your "lasso."

To begin (Picture A), grasp one end of the cord between the thumb and palm of your left hand and smooth the end down so that it lies along your forefinger. With your right hand, take the cord at a point about twelve inches away and hold it in the curve where your thumb meets your palm. While doing so, hold your right hand with the fingers pointing upward.

The first coil takes shape (Picture B) when you turn your

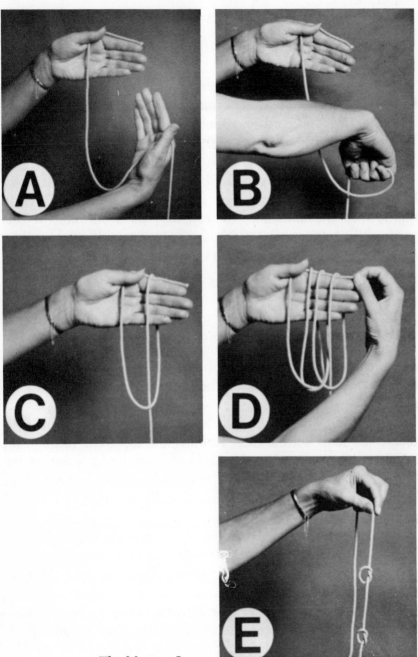

The Mystery Lasso

26043   Charlotte County Free Library
Charlotte Court House, Va.

right hand down and let the cord hang across your bent fingers. Drape the coil over your left hand (Picture *C*). Fashion several more coils in the same way and hang them in place.

Now grasp the cord end that lies along your left forefinger, and hold it between your right thumb and forefinger (Picture *D*). The cord end runs through the coils and forms the knots when you hold it and release the rest of the "magic lasso" (Picture *E*).

The ending of the trick may be varied in two ways. Instead of allowing the cord to dangle straight down, you can flick it out toward the audience. Or you may hold one end of the cord while a spectator reveals the knots by pulling the other end. No matter the ending, it's best to work with a "lasso" that's at least two feet long.

STRING RESTORAL

Audiences always expect a magician to cut a string in two and then restore it to a single piece. So that you'll never disappoint them, here's one of the simplest "restoral" tricks in magic.

Form a loop in a thin cord about twenty inches long and secure the loop with a knot. Holding the loop, cut through it. Display the cut cord with the knot now midway along its length and then pull the cord through your fisted hand. The knot disappears and the cord is magically restored to a single piece.

Begin (Picture *A*) by securing the loop with a *square* knot. The trick will not work at all well with a granny knot; the granny will tangle later on, as you're pulling the cord through your hand.

Now make your cut (Picture *B*). You seem to be dividing the cord into two pieces. Actually, you're doing nothing of the sort. Thanks to the knot and the loop, you're merely shortening the cord at one end and leaving the rest of it in a single piece. When the cord is pulled through your hand, it

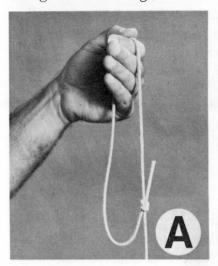
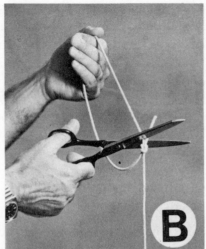
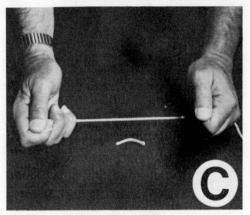

String Restoral

pops the knot open and, "restores" itself. While practicing, take a close look at how the cord passes through the knot and you'll see how everything works. When cutting the loop, you should also snip away the cord end coming from the knot.

Why? If you'll hold the cord ends and pull them while practicing (Picture C), you'll see a small piece of extra cord jump out as the knot opens. This bit leads into the cord end, and the smaller it is, the easier it is to handle when completing the trick.

When displaying the knot to the audience, keep some slack

in the cord so that the spare piece doesn't pop out for all to see. Finally, place the knot in your right palm, let it break open as you pull the cord, and then hold the spare piece concealed while you display the restored cord.

You can end the trick by placing the knot in your mouth rather than in your hand. Break the knot by pulling the cord ends. Catch the spare piece between your teeth and hold it there until you can secretly drop it into your hand.

THE STRING GUILLOTINE

This is a very neat trick that takes just a few seconds to perform. It makes a fine introductory or filler routine. Thread a string through your fingers and then pull it. The string comes away from your hand, seeming to pass right through your fingers without cutting a one.

The picture tells all. Just thread the string through your fingers exactly as shown. Then hold the two dangling ends and pull them. Away goes the string, right "through" your fingers.

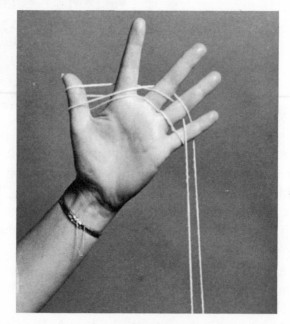

String Guillotine

THE MAGIC BRACELET

A spectator ties the ends of a cord about your wrists. With the cord stretching from wrist to wrist, you take a girl's bracelet from your table, hold it up in one hand for all to see, and then turn away from the audience. When you face front again the bracelet is seen hanging midway along the cord. It's all done in just five seconds or so.

This is the first of three tricks in this chapter that need to be prepared ahead of time. Two identical bracelets are used: the one that is displayed to the audience, and a companion bracelet that is slipped up your arm and under your sleeve. When you turn away, drop the display bracelet into the breast pocket of your coat. Then slip the secret bracelet down over your hand and onto the cord.

When you choose the bracelets, make sure that they are identical in every detail (some very sharp eyes will be watching you closely). And, of course, check to see that they'll slip easily over your hand. Press the hidden bracelet well up your arm so that it will stay securely in place until used. The cord should be about fifteen inches long.

STRING AND STRAW

Here's another "restoral" routine for your "bag of tricks." Begin by threading a string about eighteen inches long through an ordinary soda straw. Bend the straw double, hold it between your thumb and forefinger, and cut it away at the bend. Then pull the string free. Though the straw has been cut in two, the string will still be in a single piece.

Like *The Magic Bracelet,* this trick needs a moment of preparation before you go on stage. Actually, it can be prepared in either of two ways. First, you may cut about four inches from an identical soda straw, bend it double, and conceal it in your hand. When doing the trick, you then push the fake straw up and grasp it between the thumb and forefinger. It is cut while the bend in the real straw is held hidden beneath your fingers.

Or you may cut a three- to four-inch slit in the real straw. Then hold the straw so that the slit is on the underside when you fashion the bend. The string will drop through the slit and remain safely away from the scissors as the straw is cut.

And they call it magic!

THE TIGHTROPE WALKER

You don't need to say a word to bring a gasp from the audience. Just place a twelve-inch-long cord and a ping-pong ball side by side on a table. Take both ends of the cord in your hands, draw it fairly taut, and bring it up from the table. The ping-pong ball comes on up, too, and hovers on the cord—a miracle of delicate balance.

This is the third string trick requiring a bit of preparation. All you do is run a thread along the length of the cord and tie it off at each end. When the cord is held slightly taut, the "tightrope-walking" ball is balanced on two slender surfaces.

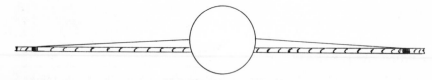

The Tightrope Walker

In the diagram, the thread is drawn with black ink so that it can be easily seen. For your presentation, of course, the cord and thread should match. Each thread end should be wrapped *lightly* into place to keep the cord from showing a suspicious "pinch." Two or three wraps at each end will be enough to support the weight of the ball. The thread ends should then be cut short and anchored down with a daub of glue. It's no fun to have an end come loose and dangle right in front of everyone. The ping-pong ball might even turn red.

Silk Magic

SILK AND STRING TOGETHER

To begin this section, let's try some magic that needs both a silk handkerchief and a length of cord. Make a loop of the handkerchief by knotting its ends together, and have someone hold it while the cord is stretched between your wrists and tied into place. Display the handkerchief (Picture A), tug the knot extra tight, turn away for the usual five seconds, and face the front again—with the handkerchief dangling midway along the cord.

The trick is done in much the same way as *The Magic Knot*, at the beginning of this chapter. When your back is to the audience, drape the looped handkerchief down the back of your left hand (Picture B). Draw the knotted end up under the cord circling your wrist (Picture C). At the same time, insert your hand through the loop. Now pull the handkerchief toward you and then away from you (Picture D). The loop will break free of your hand and slip onto the cord (Picture E).

If you wish, you can turn away again and remove the handkerchief from the cord. Just slip the loop over your hand and push it up your arm a few inches. Then insert the knotted end beneath the cord circling your wrist and pull the handkerchief down the back of your hand until it comes free. You'll be right back where you were at the start of the trick.

THE ONE-HANDED KNOT

Taking but a few seconds to perform, this is a fine introductory trick, guaranteed to capture everyone's attention. Step forward, drape a handkerchief over the edge of your hand, and then move the hand four times. By magic, a knot will appear in the handkerchief.

With your hand held thumb up (Picture A), drop the handkerchief into place: it should hang in two panels—one

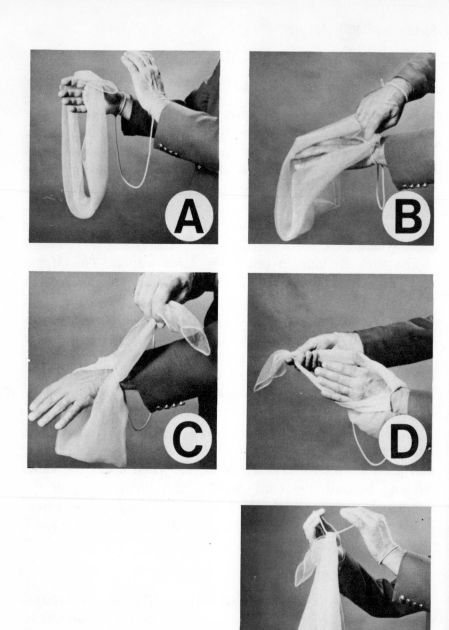

Silk and String Together

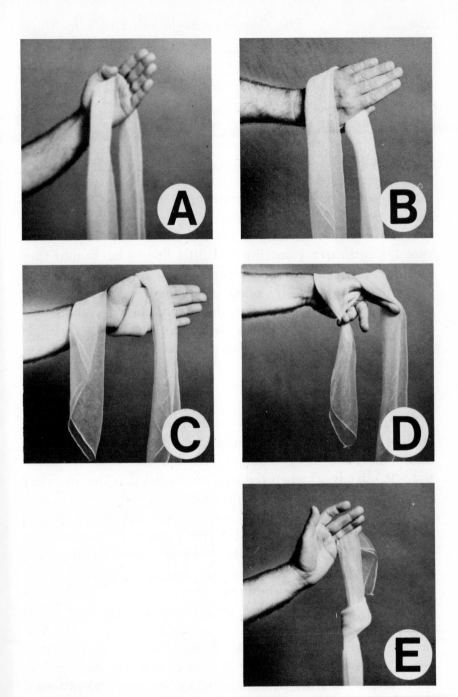

The One-handed Knot

flowing down over your knuckles, the other falling between your thumb and palm. For your first move, flip your hand over so that the thumb is down (Picture *B*). The flip should be made with some force; this will cause the panel next to your palm to flick upward, fly across the knuckle of your little finger, and then hang down the back of your hand.

Next (Picture *C*), turn your hand thumb up. You'll now have one panel draped across your thumb. The other will be draped across the back of your hand and over your wrist. You're ready for your third move.

It's the most important of the lot. Bend your fingers (Picture *D*) and carry your ring and little fingers back until they are able to grasp the panel coming down from your wrist. Hold the panel tightly, open your thumb, and make your fourth, and final, move; a firm downward throwing motion of your hand. The silk will slide over your knuckles and dangle with a knot midway along its length (Picture *E*).

THE DISSOLVING KNOT

So far as audiences are concerned, this is one of the most baffling of all the silk routines. Step forward, display two silks, and knot them together. Though the knot is pulled tight, it "dissolves" when the silks are tossed into the air. They come apart and float side by side to the floor.

You do not actually tie a knot, of course. Rather, you give the impression of doing so by first (diagram) twisting the ends of the silks together. The twist is started by throwing the end of the right silk across the left one. Then bring the left end back across the right one.

Once the ends are twisted, tie them in a single knot (photograph). Holding the ends, tug the knot to give the impression of tightening it. Though the knot now seems very secure, the twist is preventing it from completing itself and so the silks are not truly joined and will come apart when tossed into the air. Be sure to hold the ends when pulling the knot; otherwise, the silks will separate in your hands.

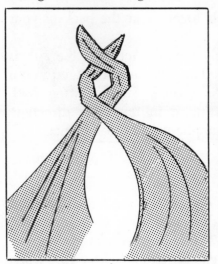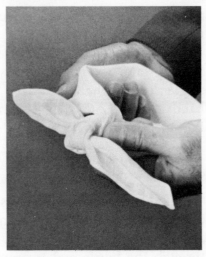

The Dissolving Knot

The toss makes a nice finish. But you can end the trick in other ways if you wish. For instance, you can dangle one·silk from your fingers; a few shakes will free the other. Or you can hold the knot out to a friend and have him blow on it; gently pull the silks apart as he does so. Or you can place the knot between your teeth and let it "dissolve" there when you tug at the silken ends.

THE SILKEN ESCAPE

Harry Houdini (1874–1926) was known in his day as the world's greatest escape artist. You may never break out of chain bindings and locked trunks, as he did. But you can still win a reputation as an escape artist by allowing yourself to be "handcuffed" with a silk handkerchief and then quickly working free while your back is to the audience.

To begin, turn your left hand palm up and throw the silk around your wrist so that the two panels cross at the base of the palm. Place your right wrist on top of your left one. Your right hand should be palm down and pointing up your left arm, toward the elbow. The "handcuffs" are completed when a spectator knots the silk panels together at the back of your right wrist.

You now seem to be securely bound. Actually, the silk is forming an 8 about your wrists. The 8 is easily changed into a single loop when your back is turned. Simply swing both hands about until they are pointing in the same direction. Pull the loop free and swing triumphantly to the audience.

SILKEN PENETRATION

To end this chapter, here is one of the most time-honored of silk routines. Drape a handkerchief over your left wrist and poke a knife down into it. The knife seems to cut its way through the fabric and is brought out from below. But when the handkerchief is opened, there's not a hole to be seen in it.

At the start, your left hand should be lightly fisted, with your fingers and thumb fashioning a cuplike opening. Once the handkerchief is in place, poke the forefinger of your right hand (Picture A) into the opening so that a little bag is formed. It is into this bag that the knife is to be inserted—or so you tell the audience!

However, as you're showing the knife with your free hand,

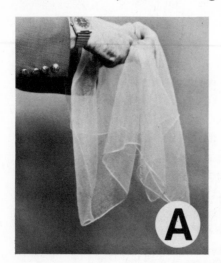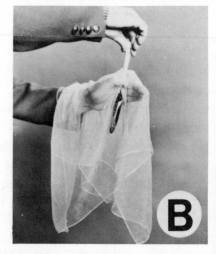

Silken Penetration

open your left fist a bit and then close it again. This movement forms an open channel (Picture *B*) that runs down alongside the bag. It is into this channel that the knife is sent. From this point on, it's all dramatics on your part. Work the knife up and down as if you're having a hard time cutting through the fabric. Make a face when the silk finally "rips"; after all, you're damaging a perfectly good handkerchief.

Hold the knife in your fist while your right hand reaches beneath the handkerchief to take it. Bring out the knife and snap the silk open with a flourish. Sweep your hand over the spot where the rip should be and then, if you wish, toss the silk to someone in the audience to prove that there is no hidden damage.

Performing Tips

1. Timing is important in all magic. It is especially important in those string and silk tricks that call for you to turn your back to the audience. Though you want to remain turned away for just a few seconds, don't try to rush matters. Perform your secret actions smoothly and deliberately. Haste will only cause you to snarl the string or the silk.

2. Make sure that your back is *fully* turned to the audience before starting your secret actions. And that the actions are completely finished before facing front again. Otherwise, the spectators are going to see some things you don't want them to see. It's a good idea to pause for a breath before beginning your secret actions, and to pause for another when they're finished. There will be plenty of time for these breaths without delaying the trick.

3. Take care with your patter. Some string and silk tricks take so little time that the audience can miss them altogether if distracted by too much talk. So keep your patter at a minimum. Never talk while your back is to the audience. You

won't be heard clearly and you'll take your mind from your actions.

4. Even though they may cost you a few dollars more, try to work only with good silks. They handle so much more easily than do cotton handkerchiefs or synthetic materials, bunching and snagging less. Perhaps you can start with one or two pieces of silk found around the house. Once you're on your way, the purchase of several quality silks at a magic shop or a department store will prove a wise investment.

5. Check to see that your silks fit your hands comfortably. The tricks become quite difficult to perform when the silks are too large or too small.

7

Coin Magic

Everyone is interested in money.

Need more be said to prove the fascination that coin magic has long held for audiences of all ages?

In this chapter, you'll find fourteen coin tricks. They are divided into two basic types. First, we'll try some that are best performed at a little distance and so should be used as part of a stage or party act. Then we'll turn to a number able to fool anyone when done right "under his nose." They make ideal dinner-table entertainments.

On stage we go.

Coin Magic—on Stage

COIN AND CARD

Coin and Card may be used as a trick by itself or as a way to startle the audience when introducing some other trick. Balance a playing card on your extended forefinger and have a spectator place a coin on top of it. Then flick the edge of your card with the middle finger of your free hand.

The card will sail out over the audience. But the coin will remain on your fingertip, ready for use in whatever trick you now plan.

COIN DEFYING GRAVITY

In Chapter 5, a card defied gravity for you by sticking to a wall. Here's a similar, coin stunt. Like *Coin and Card*, it can be used as a trick itself or as an introduction to a routine.

Borrow a small coin (either a dime or a penny), and after saying a few magic words, announce that it's now "magnetized." Then place it against your forehead. There it will remain, defying gravity, when you remove your hand.

To get away with this bit of wizardry, press the coin hard and push it upward a fraction of an inch as you put it in place. The coin will remain "glued" to your skin until a flick of your head releases it. Catch the coin as it falls and let the audience inspect it to see that you've not cheated by using a daub of adhesive. Have someone mark the coin with a pencil so that you can begin:

THE COIN THROUGH THE HANDKERCHIEF

Explain that the coin is being marked to prove that one coin—and one only—is being used in this puzzler. Borrow a handkerchief, display it, and throw it over the hand holding the coin. Now slowly bring the coin right through the fabric of the handkerchief, not causing a single rip as you do so.

Begin this very neat illusion by holding the coin between the thumb and forefinger of your left hand (Picture A) just before throwing the handkerchief into place. Once the handkerchief settles (Picture B), move your thumb so that it catches a bit of the fabric and holds it against the coin.

Next, lift the front fold of the handkerchief. Explain that this is being done to show that the coin is still there. But do not drop the fold forward again. Rather (Picture C), bring it back over the rear one.

Now comes the move that makes the trick possible. Flick the handkerchief forward (Picture D) as if returning the front fold to its original place. The flick, however, carries *both* folds forward. The coin is no longer beneath the folds but behind them, ready to be raised and "penetrate" the fab-

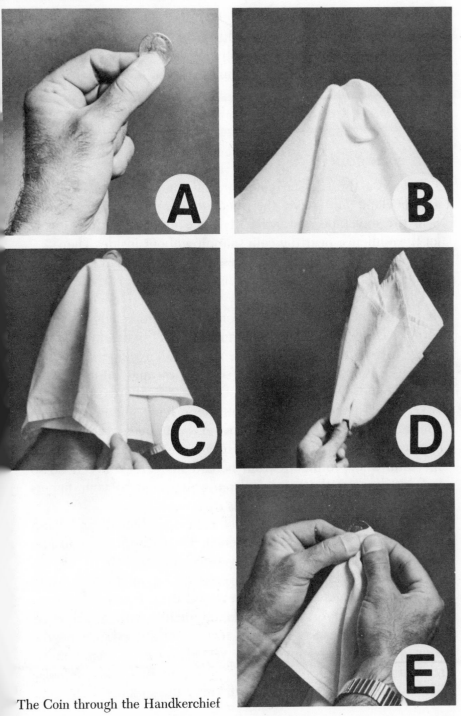

The Coin through the Handkerchief

ric. Using both hands (Picture *E*), push the coin slowly upward, apparently bringing it right through the handkerchief.

Toss the coin to someone in the audience for verification of the pencil mark, display the handkerchief to show that it is undamaged—and take a bow.

THE TORN COIN

Let's use the marked coin for still another trick. Hold out an envelope and have the spectator drop the coin into it. Seal the envelope and strike its edge against a table top to let the audience hear the coin snapping about inside. Then:

Tear the envelope into pieces and toss them into the air. The coin will be nowhere in sight.

You're working, of course, with a prepared envelope—one that has an inch-long slit along its bottom edge at one corner. Hold the slit closed and out of sight until you're ready to tear the envelope. Then tilt the envelope slightly so that the coin rolls down to the slit and escapes into the palm of your hand.

With the pieces of the torn envelope lying about your feet, you're left with a problem. How do you make the coin reappear? The possibilities are several. Why not walk to a spectator and produce it from behind his ear? You can do so just by slipping the coin up from your palm to your fingertips as your hand goes behind his ear.

Or you might pick up another envelope, seal it, and hand it to a spectator. When it's opened, there the coin is inside, having been dropped in as you were licking the flap.

If you're working on a thick carpet, you might turn away from the audience on some pretext and drop the coin. Step on the coin and pivot back to the audience with a surprised look on your face. Say that you feel something strange on the floor, and then lift your foot to reveal the coin. Incidentally, no matter how thick the carpet, the coin will make a noise when it lands. A bit of patter will cover the sound.

THE FLYING DIME

Though this trick is suitable for people of all ages, children find it especially entertaining. Just as they were delighted when *The Obedient Coins* marched out from under the drinking glass in Chapter 1, so will they be fascinated when you send a dime flying across a room and into a knotted handkerchief.

Begin by knotting the handkerchief and asking a child to hold it at the side of the stage. Borrow a dime from the audience, stand about ten feet away from the child, and have him hold the handkerchief out toward you. Tell him to watch the dime closely because you're going to toss it to him.

Grasping the coin so that it can be seen in your fingers, make three horizontal throwing motions. On the third, the dime vanishes from your hand. Without going near him, have the child untie the handkerchief. And watch his look of amazement when he finds the dime in the knot.

There are two bits of magic in the trick, and two dimes: the one that you borrow from the audience and one that you hold hidden in your hand as you prepare to knot the handkerchief.

To begin, fold the handkerchief along the diagonal between the two opposite corners (Picture A). As you do so, bring the coin up to one of the corners and hold it in place beneath the folds with your thumb and forefinger. Pulling the handkerchief out straight, twirl it into what looks to be a rope but is actually a hollow tube. Fold the handkerchief in two by bringing the corners together (Picture B). Release the dime as soon as they are joined. It will drop down the tube to the base of the fold. Finish off (Picture C) with the knot that locks the dime in the center of the handkerchief.

Now for your second bit of magic. Once you've borrowed a dime from the audience, hold it as shown in Picture D. It should be placed flat on the side of your bent middle finger and then be held there by your thumb. The ring and little fingers should be bent, and the forefinger should be extended out fairly straight.

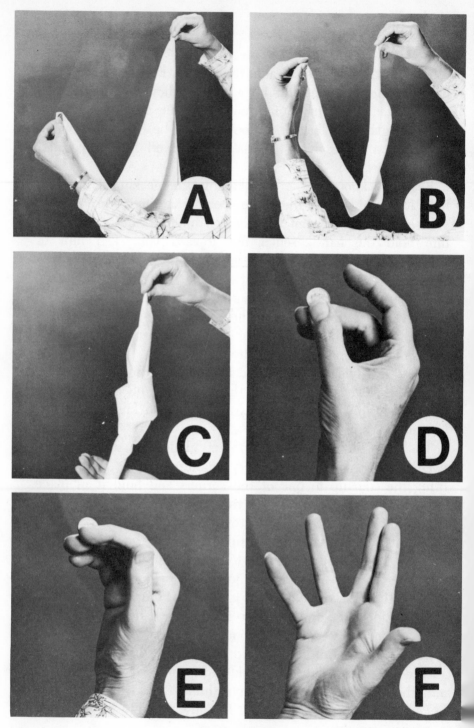

The Flying Dime

When making your first two throwing actions, sweep your arm forward horizontally. At the start of your third tossing motion (Picture *E*), bend your forefinger and bring it down on top of the dime, pulling your thumb away at the same time. Then, as your arm sweeps forward (Picture *F*), open your fingers out straight. The dime will be gone—apparently thrown with lightning speed to the handkerchief but actually out of sight between your index and middle fingers.

All that now remains to be done is to put your hand in your pocket and deposit the dime there as you have the child undo the knotted handkerchief.

THE FLYING MATCHBOX

Here's another "flying" trick. It's not at all similar to the preceding one, however. It has a mystery all its own.

Borrow three pennies, display them with your left hand, and drop one into a matchbox lying open on your table. Close the box and, after shaking it so that everyone can hear the rattling within, toss it high and let it come down on the table. Announce that the penny flew out and back to your left hand during the flight.

Prove your point by opening your left hand and revealing three pennies. Then open the matchbox and show everyone that it is empty.

To do the trick, you need a fourth penny. Hold it concealed beneath the ring and little fingers of your left hand as you collect the three pennies from the audience. Display the three pennies between the thumb, forefinger, and middle finger of your left hand. Transfer one to your right hand so that it can be dropped into the matchbox. Immediately, let the other two drop into your left palm to join the one hidden there. You're all set to reveal three coins at the end of the trick.

But what about the penny in the matchbox? How does it escape?

You guessed it. The matchbox is prepared in the same way

as the envelope in *The Torn Coin*. A slit is cut in one of the narrow ends of the box drawer. The box is held vertically in your right hand, shaken, and then tilted so that the coin can escape through the slit.

COIN IN THE WATER

Prior to beginning your act, place a half-filled drinking glass, a folded handkerchief, and a coin on your table. They should be arranged as shown in Picture A, with the handkerchief in front of the glass and accordion-folded along its length. The coin should be between the handkerchief and the glass.

When the time comes for the trick, remove the glass from the table and display it from all angles to prove that it has no hidden compartments in it. So that everyone can know that it really contains water, it's a good idea to dip your fingertips into it and flick a few drops on the audience. When finished, return the glass to its exact same spot on the table.

Take the coin, hold it above the glass, and drop it into the water. Remark that the little splash and the clinking sound prove that the coin actually landed in the glass. Next, lift the handkerchief out of its accordion fold and drape it over the glass. Now for a few magic words and the command for the coin to disappear.

Raise the handkerchief from the glass. The coin proves powerless against your magic. It's vanished.

A little sewing skill is needed to prepare the trick before you go on stage. Stitch or tie a thin thread in the hem midway along the upper border of the handkerchief. The coin is then glued or Scotch-taped to the thread's dangling end, which hangs about three quarters of the way down the handkerchief. Finish off by folding the handkerchief in accordion pleats and setting it on your table. The thread should extend to the coin from the topmost pleat.

Once your equipment is in place, you need only remember

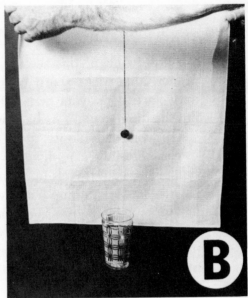

Coin in the Water

three things. First, hold the coin just a few inches above the glass when you drop it in. Watch out not to hold it so high that it pulls the thread taut and causes the topmost pleat in the handkerchief to jump. Even the slightest jump can give the whole trick away.

Second, hold the topmost pleat at the ends when raising the handkerchief. Bring the handkerchief straight up and then drape it back over the glass. Raised in this fashion, the handkerchief hides the thread from the audience.

Finally, when removing the handkerchief from the glass, take it by the ends closest to you (Picture *B*) and bring it forward and then straight up until it is clear of the glass. The coin, dangling at the end of the thread behind the handkerchief, has vanished from the glass.

As soon as the handkerchief is clear of the glass, bunch it in your hands, toss it aside, and move on to your next trick. Or, if you wish, you can secretly free the coin with your thumbnail and then make it reappear from underfoot or from behind someone's ear.

Coin Magic—at the Dinner Table

THE WRIST FLIP

Here, to begin this section, is one of the most entertaining dinner-table tricks. Turn your hand palm up, borrow a dime, and place it on your wrist. Then tell everyone that you can flip the dime over on its back without touching it.

Can you really do it?

You certainly can. Just by snapping your fingers. The action of the snap travels up your wrist and flips the coin over.

One small caution, however: Don't try the trick without first practicing a bit. The snap must be made with just the right amount of force if the coin is to flip over without flying off your wrist. You'll develop the knack with just a few minutes' work.

HEADS FOR HEADS

While your friends are still shaking their heads over *The Wrist Flip*, try this one on them. Place a quarter heads up in your right hand and then slap the hand over and down on the back of your left hand; the coin, of course, should show tails when revealed. But you're able to have it always show heads.

The trick is done by first placing the coin at the base of your middle and ring fingers. Then flick the two fingers as you bring your hand over and down to the left one. The flick causes the coin to somersault and show the heads side when revealed.

With a little practice, you'll be able to somersault the quarter easily. The somersault goes unnoticed because it is hidden by the sweeping action of your hand.

THE VANISHING DIME

Place a borrowed dime on the back of your hand and throw a napkin over it. After murmuring a magic word or two, have each guest at the table reach beneath the napkin and touch the back of your hand. Each finds that the coin has disappeared.

Murmur a few more magic words and again have each guest reach beneath the napkin. Each will find the dime back in place.

The Vanishing Dime involves a bit of "cheating" on your part. Unknown to the guests, one of them is in on the trick with you. He is the first to reach beneath the napkin on both occasions. On his first turn, he removes the dime. On his second, he returns it.

So you "cheated" a bit. It's all in the name of good fun.

BODY TEMPERATURE

This trick begins when you have several guests each drop a dime into a bowl. A friend removes one of the dimes and marks it with a pencil. It is then passed around the table, with each guest holding it fisted for a moment. Finally, it is returned to the bowl.

A guest now holds the bowl above your head or behind your back so that you cannot possibly sight the marked dime. Yet you claim that you can locate the coin just by feeling the "vibrations" of the people coming from it. And that's just what you do: reach into the bowl and produce the marked dime.

Vibrations, of course, play no part in the trick. But body heat does. As the guests each hold the coin to pass their vibrations into it, they are really warming it for you. On reaching into the bowl, you only have to feel for the one heated dime there.

ODD OR EVEN

Odd or Even is perhaps the simplest trick in this whole book. Conceal five coins in your hand and ask someone to collect a number of coins from around the table without letting you see them. Once they're hidden in his fist, tell him: "I don't know how many coins you have. But I'll reveal the ones I'm holding. If you have an even number, they'll be turned to an odd number when added to mine. If you have an odd number, my coins will make it even. Please put your coins on the table."

You can't miss, no matter the number of coins now shown by your friend. If he shows six, your five will total an odd 11. Should he have five, you'll bring the total to 10 or 12.

The whole secret is that you hold an odd number of coins. They'll always produce an odd total when added to an even number, and an even total when added to an odd number. If you wish to repeat the trick, use three, seven, or nine coins. The result will be the same.

As simple as the secret is, you'll be surprised at how few people ever sight it.

COIN IN THE ELBOW

This trick can be used at the dinner table or on a stage. Pick up a coin with your left hand and pass it to your right hand. Then place your left elbow on the table, bend your arm, and rub the coin into it. When you withdraw your hand, the coin will have vanished.

The whole trick is done at the moment you pass the coin from your left hand to your right hand. The coin seems to go from one hand to the other, but actually it remains behind in your left palm. You then rub an empty right hand against your elbow to make the coin "vanish." The false move that leaves the coin in your left palm is called the *French pass.*

Also known as *Le Tourniquet,* the move begins (Picture A) when you hold the coin horizontally between the thumb and forefinger of your upturned left hand. The right hand (Picture B) comes in over the left, with the thumb passing beneath the coin and the fingers forming a cup above it. The fingers and thumb join, just as if wrapping the coin in a

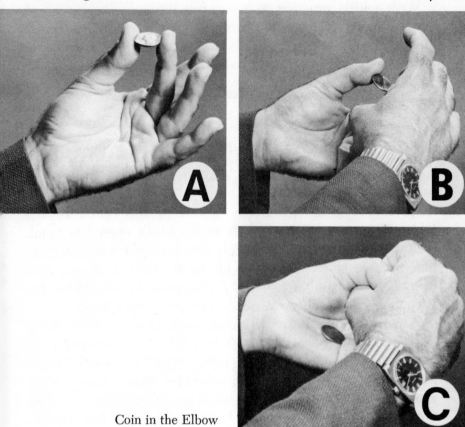

Coin in the Elbow

"tourniquet" and concealing it from view. At that moment (Picture *C*), the coin is released and drops into the left. There it stays as the fisted right hand sweeps up and away.

It's a good idea to follow your right hand with your eyes. This will cause the guests to do the same thing. Their attention will be diverted from your left hand.

Once the coin has "vanished" into your elbow, you can bring it back in the usual ways, withdrawing it from behind someone's ear or from underfoot. Or you might borrow one of the tricks from *The Flying Dime* and slip it into a napkin that you then knot and toss to a friend.

With a little practice, you can rub the coin "back out" of your elbow. While you are rubbing, let your right hand drift far over to the left of your elbow. Then drop the coin into it from above. Bring the hand back to the right, rubbing all the while, and then turn it up to reveal the coin.

FROM ONE HAND TO ANOTHER

For the final trick in this chapter, let's try another that uses the French pass.

Have the guests place ten nickels in the center of the table. Place two of the nickels in a friend's open left hand. Pour the remaining eight nickels into his right palm and ask him to hide them by fisting his hand. Take back the two from his left hand, make them disappear by means of the French pass, and tell your friend to open his right hand.

When he does, the two nickels will seem to have flown from your hand to his. There will be ten nickels in his palm.

As you've probably guessed, extra coins are needed for the trick: two nickels that are held concealed in one hand. When you pour the eight coins into your friend's right palm, drop the extra two in with them. Incidentally, have him fist his hand immediately so that he doesn't have a chance to count the coins and see that he has ten altogether. He'll never tell the difference between eight and ten by feel alone.

When you take the two nickels back from his left hand, execute the French pass just as you did in *Coin in the Elbow*. But now hold the two nickels one on top of the other between your left thumb and forefinger. And then, once your right hand has closed over your left and drawn away, open it wide with a flourish to show that the coins have disappeared. Then casually put your left hand in your pocket and drop the two coins.

All that remains is to have your friend open his right palm. Let the guests count out the ten coins and shake their heads over how you did it.

Performing Tips

1. Whenever you must hold one or more hidden coins, be sure to keep your hand relaxed and looking as natural as possible. A tightly fisted hand or stiffly bent fingers quickly betray the fact that you're holding a concealed something.

2. At times—for instance, when bringing a coin out from behind someone's ear—you must run the coin up from your palm to your fingertips. This is done by slipping your thumb over the coin and then pushing upward until your fingers can take over. The move should be practiced until it can be done naturally and easily.

3. The French pass also needs much practice. Don't forget to practice in front of a mirror. See if you can finally fool yourself.

4. As is true of all magic, timing is all-important when doing coin tricks. Train yourself to work at just the right speed. Don't work so quickly that the audience fails to understand and appreciate the trick. But don't work so slowly that they can see through to the secret behind it. Experience will show you the proper speed.

5. No matter whether you're working with coins, cards, or any other item, be sure to finish off each trick with a flourish. Never just run through a routine in "any old way." Rather, build it to a dramatic climax, helping matters along with your patter, your movements, and your expressions. Then bring the trick off at the highest point of your presentation. The applause that you'll hear will be real and you'll know that you're among those fine magicians who truly entertain and mystify an audience.

8

Mind Magic

Mind magic—or mentalism, as it is called by magicians—has long fascinated audiences over the world. Today, because people are so interested in the occult and extrasensory perception, it is more popular than ever. Audiences are charmed by someone who seems to have "special powers"—powers that enable him to see into minds, read messages hidden in sealed envelopes, and call on the spirit world for assistance. They're charmed even when they know there is a trick to it all.

Mental magic never fails to be a hit at parties. One or two good mental routines are fine additions to a regular magic act. And if you find yourself especially interested in this branch of magic, you might want to build an entire act around it. Who knows? A career might be waiting for you.

The mental-magic routines in this chapter are divided into two basic types: those that you can perform by yourself, followed by those that require you to have an assistant.

Mind Magic by Yourself

THE BURNING NAME ✕ 1

Let's start with one of the simplest but most effective mind-reading tricks. The secret behind it is so obvious that you might hesitate to try the routine for fear of being detected. But don't worry. Fire is used, and it always diverts the minds of your spectators so that they never think of what you're really doing.

Hold a small pad of paper and ask the members of the audience to call out the names of friends or famous persons. Write each name on a separate sheet of the pad, tear off the sheet, fold it, and drop it into a large bowl or ash tray. When you've collected from six to eight names, have a spectator take one of the sheets. Without letting you see the name on it, he is to unfold the sheet and show it to the audience.

Now announce that, if the audience will concentrate on the name, you'll be able to read their thoughts and call it out. With that, set fire to the papers in the bowl. Let them burn and then finger the ashes thoughtfully as if searching for the name in them.

From your expression, the name seems to take shape there in the bowl, transferred from the minds of the audience to the ashes. At last you see it clearly. Slowly call it out. Let's say that it's *Franklin D. Roosevelt*. It's the very name written on the sheet held by your friend.

By just reading about the routine thus far, can you figure out the trickery behind it? Remember, it's so obvious as to be laughable.

All that you do is write down the first name called out from the audience, in this case *Franklin D. Roosevelt*. Then continue to write that name on every sheet, regardless of the names now called by the audience. No matter what sheet is then taken from the tray by your friend, it will be the right one for your purposes.

THE BURNING NAME #2

In this version of *The Burning Name*, you read the mind of just one person in the audience. He writes the name of a friend or a famous person on a piece of paper. You tear the paper into bits, set them afire, and then call out the name.

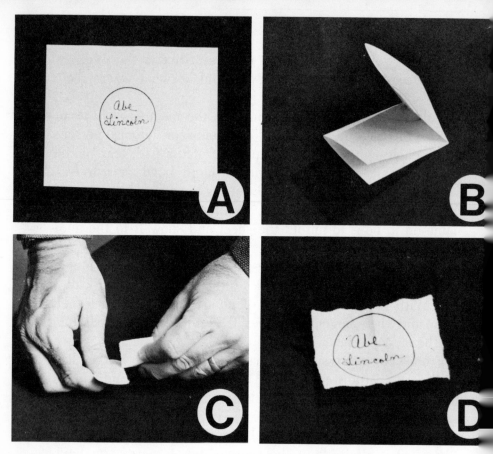

The Burning Name #2

Needed is a sheet of paper that is about five or six inches long and about three or four inches wide. As seen in Picture A, start by drawing a circle on the paper. The circle should be no more than an inch and a half in diameter.

Have the spectator write the name in the circle while your back is turned. Remaining turned away, ask him to fold the sheet twice down its middle (Picture B). He is to fold it first along its length and then along its width.

At this point, the paper is returned to you. Making sure that all the audience can see what you're doing, tear the folded sheet in half (Picture C) and place the half with the *center corner* under the other half. Now tear the two pieces in half once more; again, place the pieces with the center corner under the others. Now it's time to turn and walk to your bowl. Drop the pieces into it and set them alight. As the flames die, peer thoughtfully into the ashes and at last call out the name.

It all seems very mysterious unless you know the secret behind the routine. Let's say that the pieces of paper, after being torn, are in your right hand; as you turn to the bowl, slide the bottom piece—the one with the center corner—into your left hand and hold it hidden there while you drop the others into the bowl and set them afire.

Next, there's one more movement that you must make. While the pieces are burning, walk about the table in deep concentration, now and again turning your back to the audience. On one turn, open the paper in your left hand. On another turn, glance down quickly. There the circled name will be for you to see (Picture *D*).

Once you've called out the name, slip the bit of paper into your pocket. Don't carelessly leave the evidence on the table for someone to find later.

THE TALKING PENNY

Now here's a mind-reading routine with a "switch" to it. You do not do the mind reading yourself. Rather, it is done by a penny that, so you tell everyone, is blessed with magic powers. When hidden between two saucers, it taps out the number of spots on playing cards held up by members of the audience.

This routine never fails to charm small children, especially if you introduce the coin with the proper tone of mystery in your voice. You might add to the fun with a brief story of how the penny was given to you one dark night by an old magician.

After introducing the penny, fan a deck of cards and ask several members of the audience to take one each, but to keep the cards a secret so that the magic coin "hears" nothing. Drop the penny in a saucer and place a second saucer face down on the first. Holding the saucers firmly together with both hands, display them to the audience to prove that the penny cannot possibly "see or hear a thing."

Now move to the first child who took a card. Ask him to hold it up for all to see. Call to the magic coin, ordering it to tap out the number of spots on the card. Let nothing happen at this point. Say that the penny doesn't seem "to be picking up the thought waves just yet." Have the whole audience concentrate on the number of spots. . . .

Suddenly there is a loud metallic noise from within the saucers. The coin, as if jumping up and down, raps out the number of spots. Watch for the wide-eyed look of wonder on the face of the child with the card.

The secret behind the trick is obvious: you're tapping the bottom of the lower saucer with your forefinger or your fingernail. But it just doesn't seem possible. The sound is much too loud for that. And much too much like the sound made by the penny when you dropped it in the saucer.

The fact is, you've got some "help." Professional magicians employ a false fingertip made of plastic; fitted over the tip of the index finger, it produces a sharp sound when it strikes the saucer. You can invest in a false fingertip if you wish, but you'll do just as well by Scotch-taping a small metal washer or a B-B shot to the face of your forefinger tip. You'll be surprised and amused by the amount of sound produced.

Of course, keep your forefinger well tucked in against your palm as you introduce the routine and hold the cards out for the children to take. Then keep it safely hidden beneath the saucer. As soon as the trick is finished, casually slip your hand into a pocket and peel away the tape with your thumb-nail.

Mind Magic with an Assistant

There are many routines in mentalism that simply cannot be performed without the help of an assistant. For instance, in some presentations, members of the audience come on stage while you are blindfolded. The assistant is a "must." For who else is there to supervise the "visiting" spectators, place them where they belong on stage, and help them to play their parts in the trick?

In other routines, you stand blindfolded on stage and name the items held up by members of the audience; the assistant is needed to circulate through the audience and select the various items to be displayed. At still other times, when you are not blindfolded, the audience writes secret messages that you must answer; the assistant handles the messages, keeps them well away from you, and proves to everyone that you have no chance to peek at whatever is written. Finally, in a number of routines, the assistant adds to the mystery of it all by becoming as much of a mind reader as you yourself.

You may at first hesitate to try routines that need help, thinking that it will be too much trouble to train an assistant to do his or her part. Granted, it will be much work. But the results will be well worth the effort. When properly done, mind magic with an assistant is especially striking—and full of fun for both you and your helper.

Here now are some routines in which the assistant works in all the ways mentioned above. Let's start with one that calls for the assistant to supervise spectators who are asked to come on stage.

COLOR SENSE

The routine begins when your assistant escorts four spectators to the stage. While they watch closely to see that no trickery is involved, the assistant blindfolds you (and there is no trickery here; you really are blindfolded and can see nothing). Then, while you stand with your hands behind your back, the assistant produces a box of crayons. Each spectator chooses a crayon and holds it up to the audience.

Now it's time for you to explain the point of the routine: Each spectator is to concentrate on the color of the crayon he holds. The thought vibrations of all four people will pass into the crayons. You will take the crayons, "pick up" those vibrations, and name the colors for the audience. Though you are blindfolded, you plan to remove any last doubts that you can see; the crayons will be given to you behind your back.

Now the assistant positions the four spectators in front of you (actually, a bit to the side so that the audience has a clear view of what is going on). The first spectator walks behind you, places his crayon in your hands, and returns to his place with the others. You hold the crayon and "concentrate" on receiving its vibrations, after which you extend it to the front so that the spectator can take it. Repeat the same procedure with spectators two, three, and four. When returning each crayon, it's a good idea to have it hidden in your fist; remember, you want no one to doubt that you're unable to see.

After all the crayons have been returned, have the four spectators hide them behind their backs. Your assistant removes the blindfold and you step forward to tell the audience that the vibrations are now in your fingers and that you must now pass them into your mind. Make a fist of your left hand and raise it to your forehead so that the back of your thumb rests between your eyebrows. Concentrate deeply, and then:

Slowly and deliberately call off the four colors in the order that the crayons were given to you. Have each spectator hold up his crayon when its color is called.

All this staging hides a very simple trick. When you take each crayon behind your back, you do no more than mark its color vertically or horizontally on the nail of your left thumb. If you mark horizontally, make the first mark down by the cuticle and then put each succeeding color a little higher up.

When you then bring your left fist to your forehead, you seem to be helping yourself to concentrate more deeply. But the fact is that you're stealing a look at your thumbnail. The colors are all there for you to see and name.

HIDDEN WORDS

A very famous routine calls for the audience secretly to write out questions on slips of paper. The mentalist then answers the questions without ever seeing them. His methods for learning the questions are usually complicated and clever. But you can do much the same act with a small pad of paper and several envelopes.

While you stand on the stage, your assistant takes the pad into the audience and has several spectators write brief statements on individual sheets. The statements should be quite short, such as "I was born on _____," "My mother's first name is _____" or "My grandmother lives in _____." Each spectator signs his name right below the statement.

On returning to the stage, the assistant goes to a table on which several envelopes are lying. The envelopes are held up for the audience to see and then the statements are placed in them, one to an envelope. All this time, you remain at a great distance, not once touching the envelopes or the statements.

Your assistant finishes off by sealing the envelopes, after which you may walk to them. Concentrating deeply, hold the first envelope against your forehead. Struggle a bit as if it's a mighty task to form a mental picture of the message within. Say that you can see the words slowly forming. End by announcing the statement and the name of the person who signed it.

Then repeat the routine with the remaining envelopes.

There's secret trickery, of course. Each envelope is prepared beforehand by cutting a small flap in its face. When you hold the envelope close to your forehead, lift the flap with your thumb and read the sentence and the name of the writer.

You need to keep a number of points in mind when performing the routine. First, give the audience small pieces of paper on which to write; then the papers will fit into the envelope so that the messages are directly behind the flaps.

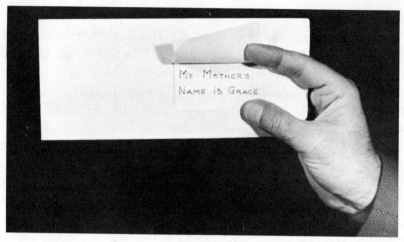

Hidden Words

Second, when your assistant shows the envelopes for the first time, a regular unprepared one should be used; it can then be set aside undetected and the message placed in the prepared envelopes. Finally, of course, whenever handling the prepared envelopes, take care to keep the cut sides away from the audience.

THOUGHT TRANSFERENCE

Here now is a routine in which the assistant also becomes a mentalist. The assistant serves as a "transmitter" to send the thoughts of the audience to the mentalist.

This is how it works: A spectator comes on stage, blindfolds you, and then remains with you while your assistant takes a large sheet of paper into the audience and has someone write a number on it. The assistant shows the number to the audience. At no time is a word spoken. There must not be any chance of the audience thinking that some sort of message is being passed to you.

The assistant returns to the stage and sits in a chair with his back to the audience. The spectator who blindfolded you leads you to the chair. You explain that your assistant will now transmit the chosen number to your mind via your fingertips, after which you will announce the number.

Place your fingertips on the assistant's temples. Slowly, just as you promised you would, call out the number.

Though not a word is exchanged, the assistant transmits the number to you by means of a code. The code: a slight tightening of the assistant's jaw, a movement that you can clearly feel up in the forehead. Suppose that the chosen number is 5. The jaw tightens five times and you have the answer.

With a little practice, the code can be developed to cover any number of any size. For instance, suppose the number is forty-three: the assistant tightens four times, pauses a second or two, and then tightens three times. Or it may be 143: tighten once, pause, tighten four times, pause again, and tighten three final times. The jaw simply tightens and pauses one more time at the beginning to increase the number to 1,143.

Zero is the only digit that can give you any trouble. But it can be easily taken care of. Some mentalists like to use ten quick tightenings as the code signal for zero. Others like to have the assistant scrape the teeth from side to side once or twice. The scraping can't be felt clearly, but it can be just barely heard.

BLINDFOLDED MENTALISM ⚡1

One of the most time-honored routines in mind magic is the one in which the mentalist stands blindfolded and calls out the names of items presented to his assistant by members of the audience. The assistant moves from spectator to spectator, takes one item at a time, holds it up, and asks the mentalist to identify it. Quite often, it is the assistant who is blindfolded on stage, with the mentalist working down in the audience and "transmitting" the names of the items via his "thought waves."

If you plan to attempt this type of magic, you and your assistant will need to develop and memorize a code. The code consists of words and phrases that cover the various items possible for the audience to produce. The words and phrases are fitted casually into the patter used by the performer in the audience. For instance, the performer might say "thank you" to a woman presenting an item from her purse; it sounds like nothing more than a courteous statement; actually, it's the performer's code signal for a lipstick or compact. Or the performer might say, "Thank you very much"—the signal that the item is a comb.

Other examples of the code signals might be:

"What do I have here?"—a ring.

"I'm holding this item quite high. Do you get an impression of what it is?"—a signet ring.

"Do you get a clear impression of what it is?"—an engagement ring.

"Do you get a strong impression of what it is?"—a wedding ring.

"Please concentrate a bit harder."—a wallet.

These are very simple examples of possible code signals. A professional mentalist's code is quite extensive and complicated, covering a vast array of items. Pauses in a sentence and changes in the inflections of the voice even play a part in it. The code takes many years to develop and perfect.

But don't let the idea of an extensive and complicated code discourage you. You and your assistant can start by working up a code that covers perhaps only fifteen or twenty items. As modest as it may be, it can prove quite workable if you limit the types of items that the audience can present.

For instance, let's say that your code is to cover only the things found in purses and wallets. You can easily guess at the items that will be produced, and so into the code they go. Then your assistant, seeming to select various items at random when they are raised during the performance, needs to pick only those on the list, ignoring all the others.

BLINDFOLDED MENTALISM ✂2

The code is necessary if you plan to work on stage at church, club, or school functions or in amateur productions. But if you're planning to limit your mind magic to parties, here's a routine that doesn't need a code. You and your assistant merely work up a list of items certain to be picked by the audience—perhaps the parts of a living room and the furniture in it. Set them down in a certain order and then memorize the list. Your list might look something like this:

1.	A picture	7.	The ceiling
2.	The fireplace	8.	A window
3.	The divan	9.	A book
4.	A lamp	10.	The floor
5.	The rug	11.	The coffee table
6.	An ash tray	12.	The door

In this routine, your assistant should not move among the spectators and take one item at a time. Rather, the items should be picked all at once at the beginning of the routine. Then the assistant walks from item to item in the order that they appear on your list.

Of course, the order of the items on the list will not tally with the order in which the audience picks them. But this doesn't matter. Go ahead and follow the list. So caught up in the act will everyone be that no one will likely remember the exact order in which the items were first selected.

What if someone chooses an item that is not on the list? Your assistant simply skips over it and pretends to have forgotten it. After all, you're naming twelve items while blindfolded, and the one or two items missed will seem nothing more than an oversight.

And what if the audience fails to pick an item on the list? Have your assistant point it out anyway. The assistant can cover the trouble spot here by saying that the item is being pointed out to make things a bit more difficult for you and to give your mental powers an extra test. Or the assistant may make sure that a missed item is picked by seeming to help a hesitant guest to make a choice. The assistant, whispering of course, suggests that the overlooked item would be a good one.

NAME THE CARD

Thus far, we've talked about routines that must be rehearsed by you and your assistant before they can be presented. To end the chapter, let's try one that needs hardly any preparation at all. It's an ideal "spur-of-the-moment" trick for parties. All you have to do is pick a friend as an assistant, draw him aside, and pass on a few whispered instructions. Just don't let anyone else know that the two of you are working together.

The trick is centered about three cards that you place in a row on the dining-room table. While your back is turned, a guest touches one of the cards. You face the table, "read" the guest's mind, and unerringly name the selected card. The trick is quickly done and so may be repeated several times without boring the spectators.

If *Name the Card* is to work, your assistant should get to the table first and sit down. When the guests crowd around, you spread the cards in front of him while he sits with his arms casually folded on the table and his hands doubled into fists. Without once speaking, he signals the position of each selected card.

When the card to your left is selected, your assistant unbends the forefinger of his left hand and rests it against his right upper arm. The right forefinger is extended to signal the card to your right. Both fists closed means that the center card is the selected one.

The trick can be just as easily worked if your assistant can't find a seat at the table. Just let him stand with arms casually folded. Some assistants like to use a toothpick, signaling by moving it slowly from one side of the mouth to the other.

Performing Tips

1. When performing as a mentalist, do not attempt to convince the audience that there is any magic involved in what you are doing. In regular tricks, you can accent the idea of magic, but now be quite straightforward in your manner, just as if you *are* blessed with the ability to read minds. This attitude makes your presentation all the more effective. Most people, though they know there must be some trickery behind the routines, like to think that mind magicians actually do have extrasensory powers.

2. Choose your assistant as carefully as possible. Try to pick someone, either a boy or a girl, who is as interested in magic as you are. Only such a person will want to put in all the rehearsal time necessary to learn and perfect your routines.

3. Pledge your assistant to secrecy as to the trick that makes each routine possible.

4. Never treat your assistant as simply a helper. Rather, remember that the two of you are equal partners. The audience and your assistant will appreciate this attitude.

5. Don't be too ambitious when first developing a code for blindfolded mentalism. Start with just a few code phrases and memorize them thoroughly. If your code is too complex, it's apt to fly out of mind right in the middle of a performance. Add new phrases to it as you gain experience and confidence.

9

Toward Advanced Magic

Thus far, we've tried 94 tricks, puzzles, games, and stunts. They've ranged all the way from the very simple *Restless Napkin* to the complicated *Blindfolded Mentalism* ⚔1, and from routines that can be performed "on the spur of the moment" to those that need some preparation. With them, you'll be able to entertain on stage or at parties for many years to come.

But suppose that you want to do more with your magic. Suppose that you'd like to become a professional magician or a very accomplished amateur who is paid to appear before local organizations. You can use many of the routines that you've already learned. But to be truly amazing, you'll want to add to them a more advanced kind of trickery.

Advanced magic is the sorcery that enables a magician to pop live animals out of a hat, pluck cards and coins from the air, and vanish anyone or anything—from an assistant to an automobile—from the stage. It's a magic that demands many skills. Chief among them are the abilities to use the hands deftly and work with special equipment.

To start you on the road to this magic, here are the final six tricks in the book. All are routines long used by professional magicians. The first three are done by sleight of hand. They are followed by a trio that can be performed only with certain equipment.

Sleight-of-Hand Magic

Sleight of hand is the name for those many secret actions that enable you to do such things as tie magic knots or move cards from one place to another in a deck. Throughout this book, you've had the chance to practice some simple sleight-of-hand movements. Now let's try a more demanding kind, working first with cards and then with string and coins.

THE SISTER ACES

To start the fun, hand the two red aces to a spectator. Have him return them to the deck, making sure that he places them at points widely separated from each other. Explain that they're "sisters" who can't bear to be apart. Sympathetic magician that you are, tap the deck to bring them back together. Then begin dealing cards onto the table. Very soon, the two aces appear—magically one after the other.

The Sister Aces is a combined sleight-of-hand and key-card trick. Let's start with the key card:

After handing the red aces to the spectator, shuffle the deck thoroughly and catch a glimpse of the *top* card; let's say that it's the *six of clubs*. Next, cut the deck roughly in half, placing the top half to the right on your table, the lower half to the left. Have the spectator place one ace face down on the right pile; this puts it directly above your key six. The second ace is inserted into the middle of the left pile. Bring the deck back together again by placing the left half on top of the right half.

At this point, you know that the first ace is directly above your key six and that the second ace is somewhere above them. It's time for your patter about the aces being sisters who can't bear to be apart. Tap the deck to bring them together.

Now take the deck and hold it face down in your left hand as shown in Picture A. With your right hand, draw the cards out one at a time from the bottom and drop them face

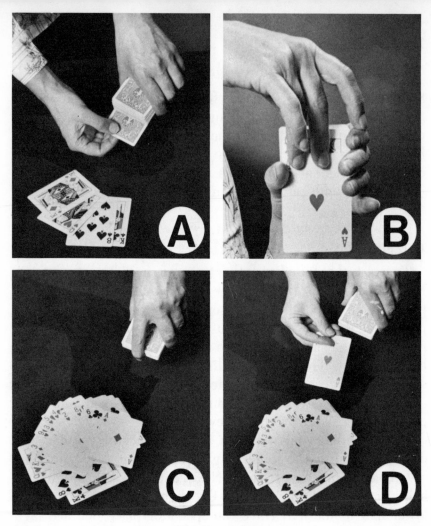

The Sister Aces

up on the table. Draw each card out by placing your middle and ring fingers beneath it and then sliding it forward.

At last, your key six appears. You know that the next card in line is the first red ace. Now for your sleight-of-hand move:

As your fingers go beneath the ace, do not draw it forward. Rather (Picture *B*), slide it back about half an inch. This action passes unnoticed if you've been drawing the cards off with your middle and ring fingers all the while. And if you've been holding the deck as you should, the moved ace will be well hidden beneath the heel of your palm. With the ace safely out of the way, continue to draw off cards until the second ace appears and is dropped on the table (Picture C).

One last secret movement remains. Tap the deck to make sure that you've exerted "enough magic" to bring the aces together. As you do so, slip your left forefinger over the front edge of the deck (Picture C) and slide the deck back until it is square with the ace. The tap hides this action. Then finish everything off by bringing out the ace (Picture D) and dropping it triumphantly on the table.

Incidentally, the aces come out in an order reversed to the way they were put in the deck. But there's no need to worry. No one ever notices this little "peculiarity."

THE MYSTERY KNOT

A real test of the nimbleness in your fingers—that's what magicians call *The Mystery Knot*.

Begin by stretching a lightweight cord of about eighteen inches between your hands. Let a spectator see that it doesn't have a single knot anywhere in it. After uttering a few magic words, toss it over his head so that it drapes itself about his neck and shoulders. Then have him hold its ends while you gesture magically and demand that it tie a knot in itself. Finish off with a dramatic clap of your hands and tell the spectator to remove the cord.

Presto! He'll find a knot midway along its length.

The trick is performed in two steps. First, you must hold the cord in a certain way. Then there's a lightning-quick sleight-of-hand action in the instant before the cord is thrown over the spectator's head.

To begin, turn the backs of your hands to the spectator and hold the cord in the manner shown in Picture A. Notice how the cord dangles down over your right hand, held in place by your thumb.

Your hands should be held high, level with the spectator's

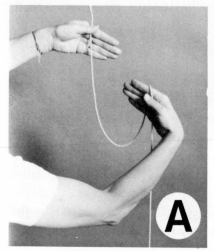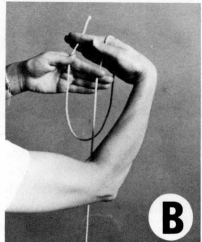

The Mystery Knot

face. In the split second before you toss the cord, bring them together. Separate them immediately and make the toss. In that brief moment when your hands meet, you actually fashion the knot. You do so by transferring the cord ends from one hand to the other.

The transfer (Picture *B*) is made by taking the right portion of the cord between the index and middle fingers of your left hand. The left end is grasped between the index and middle fingers of your right hand. When your hands fly apart, the ends cross each other in such a way as to form the knot.

The movement must be made swiftly. If so, the spectator will blink and likely miss it altogether. Or he'll think that you can't possibly be doing anything to the cord because your hands brush together so lightly and separate so quickly.

Once the sleight-of-hand action has hidden the tying action, the knot remains unseen by the spectator, for it now flies over his head and lands at the back of his neck. The magical gestures, the demand that the cord tie a knot in itself, and the final clap of your hands are just "window dressing" meant to finish the routine off dramatically.

THE MONEY MULTIPLIER

A spectator is not called to the stage for this trick. Just stand in front of the audience and amaze everyone by plucking coins here and there from the air and tossing them into a small bucket.

You need a supply of thirteen coins of the same denomination, plus the small bucket. The bucket should be metal so that the coins can be clearly heard as they land in it. A child's sand bucket, covered on the outside with colored paper, is a good and inexpensive choice. As for the coins, you'll find it best to work with quarters or fifty-cent pieces. Either is just the right size for the sleight-of-hand move that makes the trick possible.

Divide the quarters into two six-coin stacks, concealing one stack in the left pocket of your jacket or slacks, and hiding the other in your left hand. The thirteenth coin is held in your right hand. But held in a special way.

The special grip is needed because you do not actually pick various coins out of the air. Instead, the one in the right hand is used again and again. It is held flat (Picture A) in the crotch formed by the thumb and index finger and is easily hidden from view by lightly fisting your hand. It is also within easy reach of your index and middle fingers. When you wish to "pluck" it from the air, catch it between the tips of the two fingers (Picture B) and open your hand (Picture C). The coin disappears when your fingers close, returning it to the crotch.

To perform the trick, first be sure that the coins hidden in your left hand are placed in a comfortable roll. Display the bucket with your left hand to show that it is empty. Hold the bucket (Picture D) by the lip, with your hand—and the hidden coins—well inside it. Now swing your right hand up and out and pluck a coin from the air.

Finish the swing by bringing your hand down and placing it in the bucket, as if dropping the coin there. Immediately fist your hand and return the coin to the thumb crotch. Open the forefinger of your left hand and release one of the six

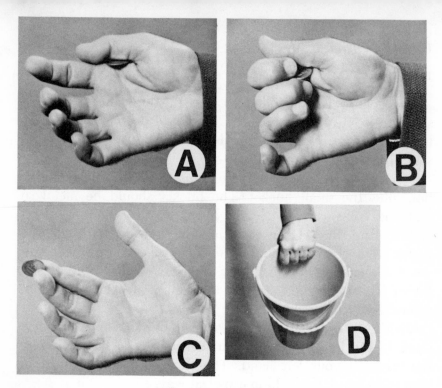

The Money Multiplier

coins. As soon as the coin is heard striking the bottom, remove your right hand and "pluck" another quarter from the air.

Once all the coins are gone from your left hand, pass the bucket to the audience for inspection. Dip into your pocket for the second stack of coins and continue the trick. If you hide additional stacks of coins in your clothing, you can keep on performing until the bucket contains two or three dozen quarters.

Equipment Magic

Professional magicians often use costly and complicated equipment to bring off their miracles. This is true of the equipment used in the following tricks when they are performed professionally. But it has been modified for our purposes. It has been much simplified so that you can make it at home for little or no cost. You'll have the experience of working with the equipment without running up your own personal "national debt."

The tricks are each explained in three steps. First, we'll list the equipment. Then, we'll talk about how it is prepared. Finally, we'll see it at work on stage.

RABBIT IN THE BOX

Let's begin with one of the most famous of routines: the one in which the magician produces a live rabbit from a hat, a box, or his coat. Live rabbits are quite difficult to handle, but you can still perform the trick if you employ a slight "switch." You produce a rabbit, indeed—but it's a toy one.

The method of producing the rabbit is startling. And the emergence of a colorful, bright-eyed toy is always amusing. The routine, of course, has a special charm for children.

To perform the trick, you'll need the following six items.

Equipment: (1) a gift box minus the lid; (2) a sheet of cardboard that can be fashioned in a tube to go inside the box; (3) a piece of thin but strong wire; (4) four small metal washers or plastic rings; (5) a handkerchief; and (6) a toy rabbit just large enough to be wrapped in the handkerchief. The items are all seen in Picture A.

Preparation: The best gift box is a squarish one. Its sides should be twelve inches long, and its depth between ten and twelve inches. To give it a nice look for the stage, cover it with colored tissue paper. Or paint it with stars or any "magical symbols" that come to mind.

Poster or illustration board of a color to go with the box will serve well as the tube. It can be purchased inexpensively at any stationery shop or in many dime stores. Choose a sheet that is long enough to be formed into a tube almost as wide as the box; if the box is twelve inches wide, the tube should have a diameter of eleven inches. In depth it should be two inches shorter than the box, so that it is completely

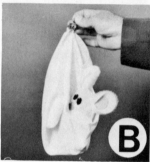

Rabbit in the Box

out of sight when placed inside. Once the tube is formed, seal its ends together with transparent tape.

Incidentally, avoid using construction paper for the tube, even though you may have several sheets around the house. It isn't strong enough. As you'll see in a moment, the rabbit is hidden from view inside the tube. The toy hangs from a hook attached to the tube's upper edge, and the weight is enough to cause construction paper to bend inward.

The hook is made from the piece of wire. The wire should be from two to three inches long and should be fashioned into an S shape. So that it cannot possibly be seen when attached to the tube, you may want to paint it the same color as the illustration board. A very thin wire, however, is practically invisible even when not painted.

Your last job is to sew the four rings to the corners of the handkerchief. Place the rabbit in the handkerchief, pull the sides up to form a sling cradle, and suspend the handkerchief by attaching the rings to the lower curve in the S hook (Picture B). The toy hangs concealed when the S hook is slipped over the upper edge of the tube.

Performance: Begin by introducing the box. Remove the tube and place it on the table so that you can display the box and prove to all that it's empty. You might even hand it to someone to check for hidden compartments. When removing the tube, be sure not to tilt it and reveal the cradled rabbit inside.

Using the same caution, return the tube to the box. Snap your fingers as if impatient with yourself and say, "Oh, I'm sorry. I forgot to show you that the tube is also empty."

Of course, you haven't forgotten a thing. For as you're speaking, one hand is pulling the S hook free of the tube and dropping the cradled rabbit to the bottom of the box. In the next instant, bring out the tube for display. To remove all doubt that it's not "rigged" in any way, why not extend an arm through it?

Back into the box the tube goes. And down through its center you reach to pull the four rings free of the S hook and open the handkerchief. This action can be covered with a surprised "Well, what do we have here!" Slowly bring the rabbit into view—and be ready for the pleased laughter of your young audience.

THE SILKEN RAINBOW

The Silken Rainbow can be performed without saying a word. Display a tube, show the audience that it is hollow throughout, and push three white silk handkerchiefs into one end. A few magic words are murmured—and from the opposite end you withdraw three handkerchiefs, all of different colors.

Equipment: (1) three white silk handkerchiefs and three colored ones, all of the same size; (2) a sheet of construction paper 8"×11"; (3) a mailing tube 2" to 3" in diameter; (4)

a piece of ribbon 4″ long; and (5) a sheet of poster board 11″×14″.

Preparation: The trick employs two tubes, one hidden inside the other. The outer tube is made by shaping the construction paper along its length until it forms a cylinder that can be slipped down over the mailing tube; seal down the ends of the cylinder with transparent tape. The inner tube is made by cutting a five-inch length from the mailing tube.

The inner tube is used to conceal the colored handkerchiefs until you're ready to produce them. They're held in place by the ribbon, which, as in the drawing, is taped to the inner wall of the tube and hangs suspended across the lower opening. The three handkerchiefs are pushed into the tube until they disappear from sight and rest against the ribbon.

The inner tube itself must never be seen and so needs a hiding place. The poster board provides that hiding place. Fold it along its width, place it in an upside-down V on your table, and set the tube behind it. Decorate the board in any way you wish and drape the white handkerchiefs across it so that the audience is fooled into believing it's nothing more than a display stand. When you're ready to perform, your equipment should look as it does in the photograph.

Performance: Display the outer tube in your right hand. After proving to the audience that it is hollow all along its length, reach for the first of the white handkerchiefs with your left hand. At the same time, lower the tube until it slips over the inner tube. Bring it up again, tightening your grip so that the inner tube remains locked inside. Insert the first handkerchief into the top with the fingers of your left hand. Then poke it the rest of the way down with a pencil or a "magic wand."

(The wand, a standard piece of equipment for most magicians, can be easily cut from a piece of spare dowel. It should be about ten inches long and one-fourth to three-eighths inch in diameter. It should be painted black, with one-inch white stripes circling its ends.)

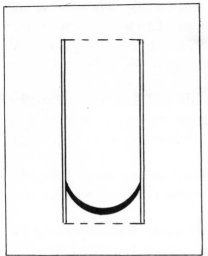

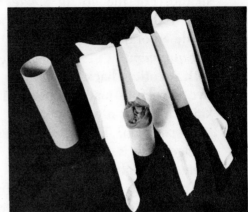

The Silken Rainbow

Push the handkerchief down until it rests firmly against the colored ones. Then reach into the lower end of the tube, slowly withdraw the first colored handkerchief, and drape it across your display stand. Follow the same procedure until the final colored silk is removed. You can now bring the trick back to its starting point by inserting the colored handkerchiefs into the tube one at a time and withdrawing the whites.

As the last handkerchief is returned to the display stand, lower the tube behind it and release the inner tube. Toss the outer tube to a spectator. Let him open it and show everyone that it contains not a single hidden compartment.

THE ACE IN THE ORANGE

The equipment used in this, our final trick, is quite simple. The accent is on something equally important: careful preparation. There's some very precise work involved here.

But the effort is more than worth while. *The Ace in the Orange* never fails to leave audiences gasping. And well they should. For the *ace of spades* is torn into small pieces and then is found put back together again—all neatly rolled up inside an orange.

Equipment: (1) a deck of cards and two aces of spades with identical backs; (2) three fresh oranges on a plate; (3) two envelopes made of tan and thickish paper; (4) a kitchen knife; and (5) a wastebasket.

Preparation: The trick is prepared in two steps. First, the orange that is to contain the "restored" ace is readied, and then, a special envelope.

To prepare the orange, carefully carve out the pip and set it to the side. Next, tear a bottom corner away from one ace —we'll call it *Ace 1* for easy identification. Don't misplace the corner. It's vital to the performance of the trick.

Shape *Ace 1* into a very tight tube by rolling it up along its length. This can be done easily if you'll first wrap the card around a pencil and then remove it for the final tightening. Now (Picture A) carefully push the card down through the core of the orange until it is completely below skin level. Coat the pip with white glue and put it back in place; wipe away any excess glue so that no signs of tampering are visible. Finally, mark the orange lightly with a pencil to avoid "losing" it when you set it on the plate with the other two oranges.

The special envelope (Picture B) is prepared by cutting away the face of one envelope and inserting it into the other envelope. This divides the second envelope into two sections. You'll see the reason for them in a moment.

Performance: At the start of the trick, the plate of oranges, the knife, and the deck of cards should be on your table. The second ace (*Ace 2*) should be at the top of the deck, and the torn corner from *Ace 1* should be in your right hand, concealed beneath your ring and little fingers. The waste basket may be on the floor nearby, or if it is small enough, on the table.

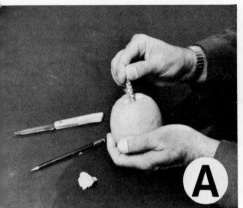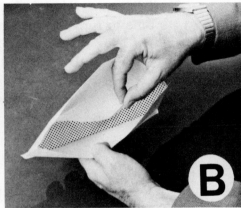

Ace in the Orange

Begin by forcing *Ace 2* on a spectator in the manner described in Chapter 4. Tear away the bottom corner for him and hold it between the thumb and forefinger of your right hand, with the torn corner of *Ace 1* hidden close by. Have the spectator now rip *Ace 2* into small pieces.

Once the card is torn, he is to drop the pieces into the special envelope. Extend the envelope to him with your left hand, with your fingers over the inserted panel so that only one compartment is visible. Then, holding the envelope up, put your right hand in as if smoothing out the pieces. Drop the corner bit from *Ace 2* in with the other pieces. Bring the torn corner from *Ace 1* up to your fingertips. Hand it to the spectator.

Place the envelope on your table. Order the pieces to vanish and slap the envelope. Pick it up, open it to the second compartment, and show that the pieces have done as commanded. Crumple the envelope into a ball and toss it into the wastebasket. With it now safely out of sight, there's no danger of the torn pieces being accidentally seen later in the trick.

Incidentally, in the section on equipment it was said that the envelope should be tan and made of a thickish paper. The color and the thickness will keep the shadows of the torn pieces from showing through as you perform.

Well! The pieces have all vanished. But to where?

It's time to turn to the oranges. Bring the spectator to your table and have him select one. If he chooses the orange with *Ace 1* hidden inside, you're all set to proceed to the finish.

But what if he picks an unmarked orange? You then must take another step or two. Have him toss his choice to someone in the audience and ask him to pick another. If he now selects the second unmarked orange, it is also to be tossed to the audience. But should he choose the marked orange, then toss the remaining unmarked one to the audience yourself. In all cases, the right orange will be left on stage and will seem to have been picked at random.

So far as you're concerned, your work is done. All that remains is to cut through the orange with the kitchen knife until you feel the blade edge against the card. Continue cutting around the card until it is all that is holding the orange. Then the orange goes to the spectator. He pulls the two halves apart, extracts *Ace 1*, and unrolls it.

And the torn corner piece that you've been carrying about since first preparing the trick? The spectator fits it to the corner of the ace—"final proof" that this is, indeed, the very same card that he destroyed just a few moments before.

A Final Performing Tip

Whenever and wherever you perform, always enjoy yourself to the utmost. Your good spirits will communicate themselves to the audience and make your work all the more pleasurable to watch.

So, no matter whether you wish to become a professional performer or simply intend to entertain your friends for as long as you're in magic, have fun.

After all, isn't that what magic is all about?

About the Author

Edward F. Dolan, Jr., was born and educated in California and has lived in that state for most of his life. After serving in the 101st Airborne Division during World War II, he was chairman of the Department of Speech and Drama at Monticello College, Alton, Illinois, for three years. While writing books for young people, he spent seven years as a free-lance writer in radio and television and was a teacher for some years after that. His first book was published in 1958, and he has written more than thirty books since then. Mr. Dolan and his wife, Rose, live in northern California, near San Francisco.

R

J